Julie makes building a profitable practice realistic by providing clear, concise directions on how to set up a financial system for your business using Profit First, while acknowledging the emotional, human experience around money and business ownership through relatable storytelling. *Profit First for Therapists* is a must-read for all private practice owners.

Maureen Werrbach, LCPC
The Group Practice Exchange
Owner, Urban Wellness

I am so thrilled that Julie has written this book. Her gentle style and simple language are so helpful for those of us who have more clinical than business knowledge, and her experience working with hundreds of private practice owners and the struggles they face makes this book a true game-changer. *Profit First for Therapists: A Simple Framework for Financial Freedom* is a must-read for anyone in private practice. Julie's practical way of breaking down the importance of profit and finances will help practices of any size be more successful and financially secure.

L. Gordon Brewer, Jr., MEd, LMFT
The Practice of Therapy Podcast
Owner, Kingsport Counseling Associates, PLLC

Profit First for Therapists is a must-read for anyone working in a solo or group private practice! I LOVED how Julie broke down the concept of Profit First and applied it to our profession specifically; I felt like she was talking directly to me and knew my business. The book very intuitively takes you through the basics of Profit First, as well as some of the advanced applications for those who already use it in their businesses.

Michelle Button, LCSW-R, PMH-C
Owner, Passages Wellness & Counseling for Women

Julie's *Profit First for Therapists* is a golden resource! Running a group practice is highly complex and not for the faint of heart, but her expert financial guidance makes a HUGE difference. Understanding and managing money properly is a must. Julie's practical steps will lead you to success versus misery.

Ernie Schmidt, LCSW
Owner, Palo Alto Therapy
GroupPracticeSuccess.com mentor

Finally, a Profit First book written specifically for therapists and the mental health profession. Many mental health professionals are chaotic in their wealth-building, accounting, and money management. With the aim of helping mental health professionals attain financial freedom, Julie breaks down and simplifies the elements needed to create financial literacy and financial health.

Ernesto Segismundo, LMFT
Owner, CAV Family Therapy

The Profit First system changed my business and life as a therapist and group practice owner! Once, I was anxious about the money coming in and going out and wondered if I would have enough to pay myself. Now I know exactly where every dollar goes and feel confident and secure about my numbers, including my very real, very stable paycheck! That's why I'm so excited to see a Profit First book just for therapists like me. Where I had to do the guesswork on my own, other practice owners now have a resource that makes this system clear and simple right from the start. With helpful hints, financial benchmarks, and how-to's for implementation, Julie's book can't be beat! I can't wait to recommend this to my consulting clients.

Kasey Compton, MEd, LPCC-S
Owner, Mindsight Behavioral Group
Mindsight Partners

This was a surprisingly easy-to-read book about finances and accounting for therapists. Because Julie works exclusively with therapist-business owners, she really has her finger on the pulse of what we need to know—even if we don't realize we need to know it. Julie takes a subject that I've often found confusing and makes it simple and easy to understand.

Lindsay St Thomas, PsyD
Owner, Lasting Wellness LLC

Life-changing, especially if you struggle with managing money. There are so many feelings (shame, guilt, embarrassment) surrounding money. This book provided me with encouragement and a foundation to start from.

Carrie Longest, PhD, LMHC, NCC, ACS, RPT-S
Owner, Healing with Play, Inc

PROFIT FIRST

FIRST

— *FOR* —

THERAPISTS

A Simple Framework for Financial Freedom

JULIE HERRES

GreenOak Press
8140 Ashton Ave., #107, Manassas, VA 20109
© 2023 by Julie Herres

Published 2023
Printed in the United States of America

ISBN (paperback): 979-8-9872163-0-9
ISBN (ebook): 979-8-9872163-1-6
ISBN (audio): 979-8-9872163-2-3

https://www.profitfirstfortherapists.com

Page design and typesetting by CB Messer
Cover design by Tehsin Gull

DISCLAIMER: The information contained within this book is for informational purposes only. It should not be considered legal or financial advice. You should consult with an attorney or tax professional to determine what may be best for your individual situation.

Julie Herres and GreenOak Accounting do not make any guarantee or other promise as to any results that may be obtained from using this content. You should do your own due diligence and consult your professional team regarding questions specific to your situation. Julie Herres and GreenOak Accounting disclaim any and all liability in the event that any information, commentary, analysis, opinions, advice, and/or recommendations prove to be inaccurate, incomplete, unreliable, or result in any investment or other losses.

Profit First can work for therapists in all countries. Because I am a US-based accountant, I discuss US tax law, entity structures, and regulations that may not apply in other countries.

CONTENTS

FOREWORD

My first meeting with a therapist did not have me sitting in a comfortable chair, watching them scribble on a notepad while participating in an introspective conversation. Nope. Not at all. My first session with "a" therapist was actually with hundreds of therapists. I was the opening keynote at The Group Practice Exchange, the first occurrence of a now-annual event that routinely brings in hundreds of participants.

Therapists and clinicians from around the country assembled to learn techniques for growing a healthy business from me and other presenters. They sought to make their practices into "real" businesses. They wished to make their companies sustainable. They craved to finally make their business serve them, not the other way around.

Typically, my speeches are preplanned. I don't wing it. I know the subject I will present, the time I have to speak, and how questions and answers will be managed. I prepare everything in advance. Not this time. The host wanted this event to be dynamic, like therapy itself. So instead of presenting what the host wanted, or what I thought people needed, I started the event by asking questions… and lots of them.

"How are you doing today?" I said to open.

The crowd gave me thumbs-ups, nods, and smiles. Some folks looked at each other while nodding and saying some version of "I'm doing great."

Looking around, I said, "Wow, two hundred therapists in this room, and everyone is 'doing great!'" I stopped speaking and kept observing the room while nodding my head in deep consideration. Then I dropped my next line.

"Everyone is doing great," I repeated. "So, that's total bullshit."

Everyone in the room laughed.

"I didn't think I would have to do this with therapists, but here we go." I picked up a notepad and pretended to be writing notes. "So, what made you say what you said?"

The group laughed again. The ice was broken. Now it was time to get down to business. I had to get a sense of the challenges these business owners faced. Regardless of their titles—therapists, clinicians, group practice owners—they are all entrepreneurs. You are an entrepreneur. And if we are going to counsel your business, you need to know what your real challenges are.

I continued, "We need to dig into the actual state of your business." I heard some murmurs. One person chuckled nervously.

"Raise your hand if you are making the money you envisioned." A dozen or so hands went up. The vast majority of the two hundred therapists in the room shifted uncomfortably.

"Raise your hand if your business makes money without you needing to do some or any of the work." About five hands went up.

Just to make sure I was getting honest feedback, I asked, "Raise your hand if you're worried about your company's financial well-being." This time every hand went up. They were being honest. They were participating actively.

I asked them to keep their hands raised. "Now raise your other hand if money (or the lack thereof) is one of the biggest stressors in your business and/or your life." Every other hand went up.

And there it was. Two hundred therapists being "held up" by a lack of money. It was clear what I needed to present that day: how to make their practices permanently profitable. I dedicated the rest of my session to teaching Profit First.

The Department of Labor reports that there were more than 577,000 mental health professionals practicing in the US as of 2017.[1] That number has only increased. And the demand? It has skyrocketed.

Are you experiencing that? Is the demand for your services increasing? Do you occasionally have more demand than you can serve? Are you a servant to your business? It is a unique dilemma to be maxed out on demand, yet not be sustainably profitable.

That presentation years ago set me on a quest of sorts. I have subsequently met with countless therapists throughout the country, learning about their businesses, their opportunities, and their struggles.

I have found that mental health care and caregiving are synonymous. The therapists I have met give everything they've got, putting themselves last—after their clients, after their teams, after everyone. Their business finances are difficult and seemingly unpredictable—cash flow slows during the holidays and summer months and then surges when, you know, a pandemic tears through the world.

Without an accounting degree, let alone general business training, managing cash flow can feel impossible. Very few of the folks I meet have any interest in accounting or finance. (I get it. I don't either.) They need a business that doesn't drain their energy or their pockets. They need a business that is permanently profitable. The need is clear. And the solution is, too: Julie Herres.

Julie and her team at GreenOak Accounting specialize in serving therapists. In their journey working with hundreds of private practice owners, they have found *the* formula to make therapy practices permanently profitable. It has little to do with the degrees, certifications, or experience of the clinician and everything to do with properly structuring the business to be consistently profitable. Julie and her team make profit a habit. They show therapists how to bake profit into every transaction and every session because profitability translates to sustainability.

In this book, Julie takes the Profit First method and perfects it for your needs. You are about to be guided, easy step by easy step, to a profitable business that doesn't require more from you. In fact, I think that by the time you read the end of this book, you and your business will be transformed. I am convinced that your business will be more profitable than ever before, you will work less, your clients will be better served, and your financial worries will fade. These are bold beliefs, but I have no doubt. Along with her team, Julie has done this for so many other therapists that I know she will do it for you, too.

And the best part? You don't need to scribble away on your notepad. Everything you need to know is already written down for you, on these pages.

It's ironic: When I asked Julie why she wanted to write this book, she responded, "I think mental health care providers need care too." She's right. You need to be cared for, too.

There is nothing more stressful than an empty bank account. Nothing triggers anxiety more than not knowing how you are going to cover the bills. That's why Julie wrote this book. She is devoted to financial freedom for each person who reads it.

And, as Julie told me, "I believe, deep down in my heart, that every practice deserves to be profitable. But not all my clients believe that, and I feel a responsibility to change that narrative."

Financial freedom does bring confidence and comfort. I know it because I have experienced both the stress of check-to-check survival and the confidence of fiscal fitness. You are about to experience the latter, maybe for the first time. By the time you finish this book, you will know Profit First is working as the financial worries start to fade away and your bank account begins to grow. You will know it when you see that your financial freedom results in even greater care for your patients.

People need to be cared for. Let's start with you.

Mike Michalowicz
Author of *Profit First*

INTRODUCTION

WHEN I SPEAK AT AN event or on a podcast, attendees often reach out to me afterward to ask how I got started in this niche. While I have my own therapist, I don't have an obvious link to therapy, like having a psychologist parent or having my life changed by a social worker as a child. I work with therapists because I am a helper at heart, but my superpower is interpreting numbers. When I review financials, I can see the story the numbers tell: the struggles, the mistakes, and the wins. I am constantly amazed by therapists who help their clients create lasting change in their lives, but I simply can't do what you do. My role in the world is to help the helpers.

Years before my firm, GreenOak Accounting, became the industry leader in accounting for mental health, we had several therapy clients. This was thanks to one of my favorite clients, Ernie Schmidt. He was happy with our work and kept sending referrals our way. At some point, the team and I realized that there was a thread of similarities among our clients who were making a healthy profit. We also saw common patterns among our clients who were struggling financially.

We dug deeper and realized that there was a formula to financial success in mental health. After we cracked the code, we shared this knowledge with our clients who were struggling and saw their practices transform before our eyes. We also used the data to reassure our clients who were doing well that they were on the right track. (Yes, even practice owners with a healthy profit wonder if they're doing things right.)

As the team and I shared this information, client after client improved their financial situation and became more comfortable with their practice and their money. We can help practice owners feel confident about their business decisions, and we can advise based on what we've seen work well in the industry. That feels really good!

On my podcast, *Therapy for Your Money*, I'm known for breaking down complex accounting topics in a way that makes sense to busy clinicians. My goal for this book is similar. In it, I give you all the resources you need to implement Profit First, a powerful cash management framework that will not only make your practice more profitable, but also give you a better understanding of the financial side of your business. I hope this will be a resource you can refer to often, no matter the size of your practice.

I interviewed dozens of practice owners as I wrote this book. Some interviewees requested that their names and identifying information be changed, but every story and anecdote in this book is true.

My promise to you is that by the end of this book, you'll have the tools and systems to grow a profitable practice so you can change your own story.

CHAPTER 1

Your Clients Need Your Practice to Be Profitable

"I CAN'T MAKE PAYROLL TOMORROW, I don't have enough money," Stacy said. I could hear the distress in her voice, the fear for her team members, her family, and herself.

For the last few years, she had been keeping her business going by seeing thirty-five clients each week, sometimes more, without taking more than a day off here or there. Her teenage son had just entered an outpatient rehab program, which meant Stacy was seeing fewer clients than usual and her community outreach efforts had fallen by the wayside. She had a hand in everything in her practice, but intakes were down, billing was irregular, and insurance payments had all but come to a grinding halt. Her team was trying to pick up the slack with a patchwork of marketing efforts, which meant that payroll was through the roof and there wasn't enough money to cover it.

Stacy had been growing her business steadily, with the hope that it would provide for her should she ever need to step away temporarily, but after all that time seeing as many clients as she possibly could each week, she had nothing to show for it. By the time she reached out for help, she felt like the whole thing was a house of cards about to collapse. She was scared, but also mad at herself. She felt like giving up.

Stacy isn't the only therapist I've met who is willing to put everyone else's needs ahead of her own. Caitlyn was exhausted. She admitted to me that she had been handling intake calls from seven a.m. to nine p.m., seven days a week, for the last four months. Her group practice had eight clinicians and a gross income of close to $1,000,000 per year, and yet she couldn't afford to hire an intake coordinator to handle the constant calls.

"Julie, I just don't think I can keep doing this," she said. "There is so much need in the community. People are hurting. I want to help them, but I can't keep going at this pace. How is it possible that I'm working this hard and I still can't afford to hire someone to help me answer the phone?"

Caitlyn had been so busy taking care of her clients and her team, she hadn't looked at the financial health of her practice in months.

"Everyone who goes into counseling is in it for the money," said no counselor ever. It's so common for therapists to want to take care of everyone else first—their clients, their teams, their communities—that I sometimes have to convince them that their practices can and should be profitable.

Money isn't good or bad. It amplifies who we are inside. I truly believe that you are on this earth to share your gift with the world. To fulfill your life's mission, you need money. I want you to have a profitable business so that you can go out into the world and do the good you were intended to do. We're playing the long game, and I don't want you to run out of cash, okay?

YOUR BUSINESS MUST SERVE YOU

YOU PROBABLY STARTED YOUR BUSINESS thinking that if you go out, serve your community, and do good work, the money will follow. That's partly true. What's not automatic is profit.

You must build a business that serves you. Yes, you will also take care of your clients and your team, but you need to take care of yourself. If you don't know where the money is going in your business, you can't do that.

It's cliché, but this is a lot like the emergency briefing on an airplane. The bored airline attendant tells you that in case of an emergency, you should put your own oxygen mask on first before you help children or anyone else around you. The same applies here. If you're burnt out or your business doesn't survive, you can't help anyone. My goal is for your practice to be profitable so you can help as many people as possible. Your clients *need* your practice to be profitable so they can have the very best version of you in the therapy room, not the version who is worried about money.

Reality check: Profit is not an event. It's not something that will happen when you finally hire another therapist, or when your revenue hits a certain milestone. Profit happens on purpose, with every session and every clinician in your practice.

One of the biggest frustrations I have with my profession is when fellow accountants tell their clients that they have "too much" profit. That phrase is usually followed by a recommendation to go buy stuff the business owner doesn't need, in order to reduce tax liability. Is there really such a thing as too much profit?! There may be more than you had planned on, and that's something to celebrate, not hide.

Profit allows you to have an even bigger impact on the community. Your work in the therapy room is so important. I'm not a therapist, so I won't pretend to understand how you do what you do. Just know that I'm constantly in awe of how much mental health professionals help to soften the hard edges of life.

When your practice is profitable, you will make a good living providing a valuable service to your clients. With each session, you will help reduce the stigma around mental health and therapy. Profit will also allow you to donate money or time to causes that are dear to you—to keep amplifying the impact of your practice.

THERAPIST GUILT

So why do so many therapists struggle with the financial side of their practice? Therapist guilt is definitely not an official diagnosis, yet it's something I encounter almost daily.

Maureen Werrbach, LCPC, is the owner of Urban Wellness in Illinois and the founder of The Group Practice Exchange, a membership program for group practice owners. Even though she now has a multimillion-dollar practice, Maureen is intimately familiar with therapist guilt. "When I first started my practice," she told me, "I had this immense sense of guilt around charging my full fee. Even though it's been close to ten years, I can still remember my lowest-rate client. I charged her

$35 per session, mostly out of fear that I would increase her financial stress as a single parent.

"Early on, I had a hard time aligning my need to be able to afford to live, and even thrive, with my duty to support my clients' mental health," she continued. "How could I be a good therapist if I was part of the problem? It took some time for me to fully accept that I deserve to be paid well for the work I do. It can be true that clients have financial stress, but that doesn't mean that we as therapists are causing it. Just because the clients have financial stress doesn't mean that I must have that in common with them."

Maureen admits that she's had to contend with several waves of guilt at different points in her career. When she established her group practice, she felt guilt around various policies and procedures she put in place, like those related to reduced rates and cancellation fees. Guilt caused her to overpay her staff at times, to the detriment of the business and its growth.

"In grad school, we learned nothing about running a business or managing finances," Maureen said. "The narrative was that the field of mental health is not about the money, it's about helping people. So as new therapists, we go out into the world and make almost nothing. It's no wonder successful group practice owners feel guilty being financially successful and can sometimes feel like it wasn't deserved or earned."

When I met with Angel Koenig, M.Ed., LPC, owner of Mindful Counseling in Texas, to talk about her journey as a practice owner, she described therapist guilt a little differently: "We go into this field to really help people, to see people through their hurt and their pain. To have to add what we see as a financial burden to that can feel like it takes away from us really being there for our client, for the relationship."

Ernesto Segismundo, LMFT, leadership coach and owner of CAV Family Therapy in California and Nevada, has been open with the mental health community about his difficult relationship with money. When I interviewed him for this book, he explained his therapist guilt like this: "In grad school, we were taught to do counseling out of the goodness of our heart and without considering money. And when you say to a suicidal client, 'My fee is $175,' it goes into a morality issue for many of us. We feel like we're responsible for helping the client. As therapists, we feel like the client is thinking, 'I'm depressed. My life is falling apart, and you're going to charge me $175 to help put it together? What the heck?'"

Therapist guilt pushes my clients to offer too many sliding scale slots. It causes clinicians to waive the late cancellation fees that are clearly stated in their paperwork. It allows counselors to trample all over their own boundaries and schedule clients in need at times that don't work for them. Therapist guilt can be insidious and all-consuming.

"There is a strong sense of obligation, that we have to give," Ernesto told me. "We have to take care of the community, and there's a big responsibility to make these life changes, to help our clients have a better life. But there's guilt, a therapist guilt that never quite goes away."

Why do I bring this up? Because I want you to look that big hairy guilt right in the eyes and tell it to back off. You are a helper, and you deserve to make a good living just as much as anyone in any other profession—or even more. You are amazing and talented, and you deserve to get paid for the healing your work brings to the world. I find it fascinating that this type of guilt doesn't seem to exist in other healthcare professions. You won't see a spinal surgeon reduce their rate because a patient can't afford it. So let's just admit that the desire to help others, which led you to a profession in mental health in the first place, might be doing you a disservice when it comes to the financial side of private practice.

If you've already done some work on your money mindset and don't feel guilty about making money, I commend you. You probably know that most practice owners aren't quite there yet. Over the years, my team and I have been part of many tearful money conversations; received countless late-night, frantic emails about anything and everything financial; and reassured clients on a regular basis. I'm not qualified to help you work through your feelings, but I do have to address the guilt so many therapists feel because I see it day in and day out, and it is a major barrier to the work that I do.

MONEY PROBLEMS

OTHER THAN AT THE VERY early stages of private practice, money problems for therapists occur in either one of two circumstances: when the number of sessions scheduled either goes down or up. When sessions slow down, you're facing a bunch of no-shows or worse, crickets on the phone. Rent is due but cash isn't coming in. Money problems can also occur when you have more sessions on the books. As the pace of business moves faster, like an out-of-control merry-go-round, it's harder to slow things down. Your payroll costs increase steadily, you need more space, and you're forced to throw money at problems to plug the holes in what feels like a sinking ship.

As a business grows, it's normal for expenses to grow as well; but when things are out of control, expenses can grow exponentially faster than income. It's a dangerous cycle to chase the next insurance deposit to pay for last month's expenses. You don't need to be stuck living deposit to deposit. It's stressful and unsustainable.

I am certain that you are an incredible clinician. I also know that—unless you're a unicorn—there's a good chance you haven't taken a single accounting course in your life. You haven't learned how to manage the money in your business, but without money, your business simply cannot survive.

It might feel sometimes like your practice is a runaway train and you're just along for the ride, but I want you to know that you and your business *can* have your happily ever after. Whether your revenue is $10,000, $100,000, $1,000,000, or $100,000,000 each year, your practice can be a money-generating vehicle for you and your team to change the world. What I'm about to share with you will make your business profitable quickly and permanently. We're going to face your financials together and make your business behave.

THE GROWTH TRAP

THE BIGGER THE BUSINESS, THE bigger the impact and, at the same time, the bigger the problems. Large businesses aren't always profitable. More growth won't necessarily fix a model that isn't working or profitable. You can't grow your way out of a problem.

Growing a profitable practice will (almost) always mean more profit. With profit built in, there's no need for loans, investors, or to "just keep growing." You grow if you want to, but you can stay exactly where you are if you prefer. And you make a profit no matter what.

I want to dispel the myth that top line revenue is the only thing that matters. The amount of money coming into the business—the gross revenue, gross income, or top line—is often used as a vanity metric. "Look at me, I have a million-dollar-per-year practice!" (Just kidding, you wouldn't do that.) As someone who has seen the financials of hundreds of private practices, I can assure you that things aren't always what they seem. Just because a practice looks successful doesn't mean that it is, and sometimes practices that look small and modest on the outside have the best profit margins. There are plenty of $250,000/year practices with more profit than $1,000,000/year practices. There are also plenty of $1,000,000/year practices whose owners work much less than the owners of $250,000/year practices.

Ultimately, having a million-dollar practice means nothing if you're broke. With the Profit First system in place, you'll be able to focus on profit. That way, if you choose to scale, your profit will scale with you.

FINITE RESOURCES

STARTING A THERAPY PRACTICE CAN be fairly inexpensive, especially when compared to other medical specialties like radiology or dentistry that require some significant investments. Those fancy X-ray machines cost more than $50,000, yet you could start a therapy practice with little more than a laptop and a few software subscriptions if you wanted to keep costs to a minimum.

Unfortunately, though, therapy isn't valued by insurance companies the way other specialties are. In many medical specialties, a lower-level technician can do most of the work while the doctor just pops in for a few minutes. With the right scheduler, a dentist can see around three to six patients each hour. In therapy, you're 100% present for your client for the forty-five, fifty, or sixty minutes you are scheduled with them. No technician, no breaks, no double-booking.

The earning opportunity for a solo practice owner with no team members is finite. There are only so many hours in the day, so other than seeing more clients, the only way to increase your revenue without hiring is to drop insurance panels, go private-pay, and raise your rate.

What if, instead, you considered how your practice could become more profitable? What if, instead of just *doing* more, you could get more done with the resources you already have?

TRADITIONAL ACCOUNTING IS KILLING YOUR PRACTICE

HERE'S THE THING: YOUR CLIENTS need your practice to be profitable, and to be profitable you must take your profit first. It is simply too important to wait for a future milestone. If you're worrying about money, you're not the best clinician you can be.

You might be familiar with the traditional accounting equation:

$$Income - Expenses = Profit.$$

If you manage your practice like most entrepreneurs, you start with income, then subtract your business expenses (rent, payroll, office supplies, software, etc.) and consider what's left as profit. From that profit, you pay yourself and taxes and, if you're lucky, you have money left over. You deserve better than leftovers.

The traditional accounting equation makes logical sense. But humans tend to make financial decisions based on emotion rather than logic.

As logical as I tend to be, especially around money, I have made some questionable purchases in my life based on emotion. Shortly after the birth of my first child, I convinced myself that I deserved a "push present." I picked out a beautiful diamond band and mentioned it to my husband regularly. When I didn't receive the ring a few weeks later, I asked him about it. He responded, "It's beautiful, but it sounds like we can't really afford it?" I have always managed the money in our household, and it turns out my husband *had* been listening when I told him we'd need to tighten our belts after the baby's arrival. He was right; our budget had very little wiggle room. Still, I responded with the suggestion that we accept a 0% credit card offer. I probably also mentioned the meager amount we had in a savings account. I really wanted the ring, and I was willing to bend reality to get it. Eventually, I did, but in hindsight, the purchase didn't make sense. Even though my logical brain usually prevails, my emotional pull to spend was stronger.

You know the feeling you get when you look at your bank balance? The one that falls somewhere on the spectrum between "OMG, I'm rich" and "Oh crap, that's not good"? It stirs something in you and evokes your emotions in ways that a financial report just can't.

Another issue with the traditional accounting equation is that it's not a true measure of cash. Many business owners learn the hard way that showing a profit on their profit and loss (P&L) statement doesn't necessarily mean there's any cash in the bank. While the report lists income, expenses, and profit, it doesn't show the full picture.

So many times, I've sat in front of a client during a monthly or quarterly video meeting and heard: "Julie, I just don't get it. If my business generated that much profit, where is it? My bank account doesn't have this much money in it." That's because a P&L only shows a portion of what's going on in the business. It doesn't show owners' draws, loan principal payments, asset purchases, or other transactions that appear on the balance sheet. The P&L report might show a profit, but that doesn't always mean there is any money left.

When you're just looking at your bank balance and doing "bank balance bookkeeping," you're not getting the full scope of what's going on in your business. In an ideal world, you'd look at your P&L and balance sheet alongside your bank balance, but years of experience have taught me that no one does. So instead of tricking you into being a sophisticated financial analyst or trying to change the way you behave, we can use this behavior to your advantage.

This is the magic of the Profit First system. It flips the accounting equation that most people use.

Traditional equation. Income – Expenses = Profit.

Profit First equation: Income – Profit = Expenses.

You'll learn more about why this works so well in the pages to come. For now, just know that this simple switch can change everything for your business.

Profit First is a system that will instantly tell you how your practice is doing, without you even having to look at your financial reports or do complicated calculations. It will show you how much you can spend in each area of your business. It will show you how much money is reserved for taxes and for yourself. The Profit First system will meet you exactly where you are and won't require you to change your natural behavior; instead, the system will work *with* it.

Profit First will allow your practice to be profitable at any size. Instead of focusing only on the money coming into the practice, you'll also focus on how much you get to take home.

You don't have to feel like the only way to increase your profit is to see more clients. If you don't want to grow, you don't have to, and you can still take your profit first.

PROFIT IS NOT A DIRTY WORD

"I HAVE A CHIP ON my shoulder about *Profit First*."[2]

When Leila told me that she was initially turned off by the title of the book, she explained that it was because she thought it would ask her to put profit above people.

"It seemed incredibly selfish to me," she explained. "And not aligned with my values."

The funny thing is, Leila *did* want some help with managing her money so she could grow her practice. After she listened to how some of her colleagues were implementing Profit First and heard them describe the system, she realized she may have had it wrong all along.

Leila decided to give the book a chance and committed to reading only one chapter to see what all the fuss was about. That's how she started to fall in love with the Profit First system. After always paying her expenses first and taking home what was left, the idea of flipping the script and figuring out what she needed in terms of profit was a revelation. Instead of thinking, *Oh, well, I guess this is all I have left, so I'll just have to make do,* she could start with her needs. That shift brought her a sense of peace, and it slowly started to replace her scarcity mindset with an abundance mindset.

Leila said, "I'm still working hard, but Profit First is almost like putting a budget and measures around the expenses of the business—for example, what I have left to spend on supplies. And I know I can get really creative with that."

Setting up a budget had felt so restrictive, but the truth is that it freed her. It gave her permission to pay herself.

For Leila, one of the biggest challenges of implementing Profit First was shifting into the mindset that her business can make a difference, serve the community, and provide for people's livelihoods, but it can (and should) also take care of her. She started her business to have a positive social impact on her community and make a difference, not to make money, but she has come to the realization that having a profitable practice allows her to have a greater impact on that community. She can achieve her family and life goals, and that feels really good. Those goals did not feel quite as accessible or justifiable before.

Profit First gave Leila the permission to pay herself and consider her own family's needs in addition to the business's needs, and that is a huge win.

Leila shared with me that addressing her own relationship with money has had a positive impact on her clients, too. It helps her show up with integrity as she helps her clients through their own money baggage.

It seems like burnout causes therapists to leave the field faster than new therapists enter it. Doing the work of a clinician comes at such a high emotional cost; it doesn't need to come at a high financial cost as well. Your practice can be not just successful, but also truly sustainable and life-giving. Therapists shouldn't need to carry a caseload of ninety-five clients, see forty sessions each week, and make just enough to survive. With a profitable practice, owners can provide a healthy environment for their clinicians and themselves so that they can do their work long-term, keep coming back to it, and stay in love with it. That's where truth and idealism come together.

MY STORY: RUNNING A SMALL BUSINESS CAN BE A STRUGGLE

I HAD A VERY HAPPY childhood in a very average, loving French-Canadian family. My mother was an entrepreneur for as long as I can remember. One of the oldest faded memories I have of my childhood is walking through the racks of colored fabrics in my mother's fabric store. The bolts were beautifully set on circular tables, standing up tall with dividers propping them up. I loved the feeling of the silks, wools, and stretchy blends under my fingers. I would circle the tables, touching every fabric as I went. (Now that I'm a mother, I can only imagine how many times my mother had to tell me to wash my hands or stop touching everything.) I would look at the wall-mounted display that held scissors, boxes of pins, countless spools of thread, and so much more. My sister and I hid under the display tables, learned to sew dolls and stuffed animals, and spent many a Saturday afternoon playing in the back room of the store.

My mother's sewing dream ended in a fire that started in the little deli downstairs. But the truth is, the dream was about to end, fire or not. The store hadn't turned a profit in months, as evidenced by my parents' numerous fights. There wasn't any money left to put into the business, and there wasn't enough love left in my parents' marriage to keep them together.

A divorce, a move to a new city, and another business later, the same cycle happened again: sales not high enough, expenses much higher than expected, and negative profit. This time, bankruptcy was the answer. (Bankruptcy doesn't solve everything, but it was my mother's answer to the problem at hand.) My father was very involved in our lives, so my mother had the advantage of having a caring co-parent with a steady job. The child support checks were always regular and covered most of our expenses. Every time a business failed, we'd have to start over: new home, new school, new friends. Change was the only constant. After a long week of too few sales, my mother would be quiet on the drive to my father's house, where she would drop us off for a weekend of fun. She would put on a smile and try to be upbeat, but we could tell that things weren't going her way. I remember looking out the window and counting the trees as my mother drove down the familiar streets, wondering why starting a business was so hard. I knew my mother was smart; why couldn't that be enough to make money?

A few years later, when my sister and I were in college, our mother came to us with what would be her final business idea. She was going to buy the phone book business in a tiny Central American country—so small that the phone book business was a one-person show. My mother showed us the P&L, carefully prepared by the owner who was ready to walk away ASAP. If the numbers were true, this was a golden opportunity. But something didn't feel quite right. As young college students (who obviously knew everything), we asked lots of questions: Is your Spanish good enough to run this business? How long will phone books really be around? If this is such a profitable business, why is the owner leaving? Are these numbers real?

As you might imagine, the numbers were not real, the business was not profitable, and the community was less than welcoming toward a single woman with who barely spoke any Spanish. The business survived one or two years at the hands of my mother, only thanks to a small inheritance she received at around the same time, and then disappeared in a slow, painful demise. By that point I was out of college, and I vowed that I would never be a business owner. If my mother couldn't figure out how to make it work, I didn't think I could either.

Fast forward several years, and I had a young family and was ready to jump back into the workforce after scaling back for a few years. I was the caretaker parent at the time, so I was looking for something flexible that would allow me to continue managing preschool pickups, phone calls from the school nurse, field trips and days off, and everything in between. No matter how hard I looked, though, I just couldn't find a remote or flexible position that wasn't actually a full-time position with part-time pay. I was slowly realizing that starting my own business could be the solution, but I was scared. I mulled the idea for weeks, wondering if I could pull it off, before I even had the courage to say it out loud.

I remember the night I said to my husband, Mick: "What if I just started my own business so I wouldn't have to answer to someone else?"

As parents of small children, it was one of our rare quiet times. I think Mick knew how important this moment was to me because he paused reflectively. He had been the co-owner of a small IT firm that does government contracting for close to ten years at that point, so he understood the weight of being a business owner.

Then he replied, "Why not?"

That's all the encouragement I needed to take the first step. I already felt at home with a P&L and a balance sheet. As an accountant, I knew in theory what it took to have a profitable business. But knowing what my mother had gone through, I was painfully aware of how things could go very wrong if I wasn't careful. I couldn't put my family's financial future at risk, so I set out to find a better way. And that way was Profit First. Including profit in my calculations in the first place was the answer to making sure my business would be profitable.

As I write this, my mother is in the final stages of her battle with ALS. By the time this book is published, she will be gone. There will be no more businesses for her, no more hustle. I can't help but wonder: Would things have been different if she'd just had the advantage of Profit First? I'm writing this book because I know things can be different for you.

CHAPTER 2

The Profit First Principles

WHAT IF YOU TOOK YOUR profit first?

Let's start by defining what profit is. As a business owner, you mostly likely work in your practice, and you should get paid for that work. You are also a shareholder. If you own stock in AT&T or Lowe's, you are a shareholder and receive a portion of their profit in the form of a dividend. This is a financial benefit you receive for being an investor. Just as a large company would pay you a dividend for the risk you took investing in it, your practice should reward you with a profit distribution as compensation for the time, investment, and efforts you have put into it. This profit is a reward and should be above and beyond what you pay yourself to sustain your personal living expenses.

Profit is not intended for reinvestment. Have you ever heard someone say, "I have a profitable practice, but I'm reinvesting all my profit into the business?" That's code for "I'm spending every dime I have." If there isn't any profit left over for you to take home, the practice simply isn't profitable.

Having a profitable business will make everything easier: hiring, selling your business, qualifying for a home mortgage, and *paying yourself*! If your profit margin is razor thin, you won't be able to jump on an opportunity when it lands in your lap. You might not be able to hire ahead, before you or your admin team get completely overwhelmed. Lenders are already more skeptical of small business owners, but if your business has little to no profit? They'll ask you (and your accountant) for a mountain of paperwork to qualify for a loan or mortgage. But most importantly, if you're not building profit into your practice operations and life throws you a curveball—such as a top clinician leaving, getting hit with an insurance clawback, or having a personal emergency—you can easily find yourself in a position where you need to use some of *your* personal funds to keep the business afloat.

THE FOUR CORE PRINCIPLES OF PROFIT FIRST

THE FOUR CORE PRINCIPLES OF Profit First are also nutrition principles. Though I'll be the first to admit that I am a financial expert and not a nutrition expert, it is true that there are significant similarities in how humans make choices about food and money, through hundreds of micro-decisions each day. The cumulative impact of each day's decisions creates the reality of our physical and financial health. The Four Core Principles are:

1. Use Small Plates
2. Serve Sequentially
3. Remove Temptation
4. Enforce a Rhythm

Let's look at each principle in more detail:

1. Use Small Plates (Parkinson's Law)

According to Parkinson's Law, the demand for something expands to match supply. I grew up in the "finish your food" generation, when it was a good thing to clean your plate. For me, that means that whether I'm eating from a large plate or a small one, I'm probably going to finish most of the food I am served. If I don't, it's because I spend lots of energy making many micro-decisions and reminding myself to not finish my plate. *Will I finish the vegetables or the starch? How much will I leave? Should I have one more bite?*

The same applies to your bank account. If you have one checking account where all your business funds sit, that account serves as one large plate. In this situation, your brain naturally thinks, *These are the resources I have available to me, so I'm going to consume them all.*

We implement the concept of small plates by dividing your money into a number of accounts. It's natural to want to do "bank balance bookkeeping." You check your bank app in the morning, see that there's money, and decide all is well. But that number doesn't account for the fact that payroll is due next week, your tax payment is due in six weeks, and your credit card payment is also due in a few days.

If all your business funds are hanging out in one account, you might feel like Uriah Guilford, LMFT, owner of InTune Family Counseling in California, who says, "If I look at my bank account at any given moment and there's a big pile of money, I feel rich. It's easy to do. Profit First protects me from myself because I can clearly see that some of that money isn't available to me. It's already been earmarked for taxes, payroll, or expenses, and I can't spend it."

When you use a smaller plate, or bank account, your business naturally consumes less. The beautiful thing about this system is that you won't need a will of steel for it to happen.

As a college student, I worked as an administrative assistant at a technology company over one summer break. I filled in for a vice president's assistant, so whatever this VP needed, I did. Need your dry cleaning picked up? No problem. Your car needs an oil change? I've got you. No time for lunch? I'll pick up a sandwich on the corporate card.

One thing I remember vividly from that job is the day my VP boss told me he was buying a bright yellow Porsche Carrera. He asked me to submit his company stock sale paperwork so that he could make the down payment on his midlife crisis car. Then he needed help to gather all the paperwork so the dealership would give him a car loan. As I put the documents neatly into a file folder, I was blown away by the pay stub I had just printed. He was making *how much* money? How was that not enough to go buy the car outright? Why did he need financing or to sell stock at all? As a broke college student, I truly couldn't fathom how I could ever make that much money, let alone spend it on a fancy car.

My shock and self-reflection must have shown on my face when I walked into his office, because he said something that I'll never forget: "Julie, when you make more money, you spend more money. The problems just get bigger." Wow.

With the distance of time, I can absolutely see how that's true. Our needs, and wants, change based on what's available. So what if we just made what's available smaller?

When we have less, we automatically do two things: one, use less, and two, get creative.

The way we use Parkinson's Law in the Profit First system is essentially like using smaller plates to eat less. If we make our bank accounts (plates) look smaller by splitting the funds between multiple accounts, we will naturally spend less and get creative when it comes to expenses.

2. Serve Sequentially

I like to use buffet lines as an analogy for serving sequentially because they are laid out very intentionally. Going through a buffet, you'll notice that the voluminous and inexpensive items, like salad or bread, are typically first. They take up a lot of space on your plate, so as you keep going through the line, you'll take a little less of everything else. By the time you get to the most expensive items at the end of the buffet, the protein, you'll have just a little bit of space left on your plate and will take less protein. If you've ever been to a buffet with prime rib, it's usually the last item on the line. It's an intentional cost-cutting strategy to put the cheapest items first and the most expensive items last.

My point is: order matters. Your brain can only focus on so many things at one time, and it tends to add significance to what it encounters first.

What you focus on tends to get done. Personally, if there's a project that I *must* complete in any given day, it's the first thing

I work on. In fact, I've written most of this book between the hours of six and eight a.m.

In the context of your practice, this means that we're going to take care of you, the owner, first. Your business must allow you to sustain your personal life. That's nonnegotiable. If you pay yourself first, you'll have less money for all the other expenses in your business—but you're going to make it work.

When we focus on profit *first*, it gets done.

3. Remove Temptation

You've probably heard that Google has amazing perks for employees, like free micro-kitchens throughout each building with unlimited snacks and drinks. In Google's early years, one side effect of all that free food was that most new hires gained an average of ten pounds after they joined the team.

After seeing this data, Google's food team decided to make it easier for people to make healthy choices and avoid the temptation of sweet treats if desired, while keeping all the current food and snack options available.

At the time, M&Ms, the most popular candy in their kitchens, was kept in big, clear bulk containers. The food team made one small change: they put the M&Ms in opaque containers and displayed healthier snacks like fruit more prominently. They didn't change the quantity of M&Ms available; they just put them in different containers.

In the New York office alone, that change resulted in 3.1 million fewer M&M calories consumed over a period of *seven weeks*.[3]

The same concept applies to money. If it is out of sight, it will also be out of mind—so much so that my team often has to remind our clients that they have money in a separate bank account earmarked for taxes. When your cash is split between several bank accounts that are named for their intended purposes, you'll naturally learn not to consider those funds available when you look at your bank balances.

4. Enforce a Rhythm

Think about the times when you're so busy that you just don't have time to grab something healthy for lunch. By the time you get home, you're absolutely starving and probably cranky (I am, at least). The times I wait too long to eat are the times I am most prone to overeating and making bad food choices.

Enforcing a rhythm with your money is important, too. As you implement Profit First, you'll transfer funds to your bank accounts on a set schedule. It will become part of your life, something you do automatically, like brushing your teeth every night. If you go too long between transfers, you'll starve your business of the food (cash) it needs to survive. Establishing a rhythm will also help you see the ebb and flow of cash in your business. Instead of looking at your statement of cash flows (or cash flow statement), the financial report that shows you how your cash balance has changed based on loan activity, credit card transactions, distributions, and more, you can see the cash flow by looking at the balance of each account. (And let's be honest, I don't think any of my clients ever look at the statement of cash flows.)

SETTING UP YOUR PROFIT FIRST ACCOUNTS

Now that we have reviewed the Profit First principles, you know that you'll need multiple bank accounts for your business. The Profit First accounts are meant to create a sense of scarcity. This method is very similar to the envelope system for personal spending, where you place cash in envelopes labeled Mortgage, Groceries, Car & Gas, etc. each week and spend only what's in the envelope, not a penny more. In this information age, when hardly anyone carries cash anymore, envelopes don't make sense, especially for a business. But bank accounts can serve the same purpose. Lots of bank accounts.

Setting up the Profit First accounts is the first game-changing domino, but it's the part of the process that my team and I tend to get the most resistance about. And that's with people who *want* to implement Profit First! As I interviewed practice owners who have implemented Profit First in their businesses for this book, one of the themes that came up again and again was: "I thought I could do it without the accounts, and then I realized I couldn't. I wish I had set them up much sooner." At the end of this chapter, I'm going to ask you to go and open additional bank accounts. I truly hope you'll take that action. My research and experience have shown that opening the bank accounts is a catalyst for the many positive changes coming your way and a sign that you're ready to commit.

There are five foundational accounts that every practice will use, plus one account that will only be used for practices with employees. In Chapter 8, I'll go over some Advanced Profit First strategies and present a few more optional accounts.

The foundational accounts are:

- Income
- OpEx (Operating Expenses)
- Payroll (you'll only use this account if you have employees or contractors)
- Owner's Pay
- Tax
- Profit

> GOING FORWARD, I'LL REFERENCE THE PROFIT FIRST
> BANK ACCOUNTS BY THEIR CAPITALIZED NAMES,
> FOR EXAMPLE, PROFIT AND TAX.

Let's go over each account in more detail.

Income: All incoming deposits will go into this account. If you plan to stay with your current bank, your checking account will become your Income account. This important step will greatly simplify the implementation process.

A note about the Income account: There is an additional benefit to seeing only your deposits in one account. It's not unusual for our Profit First clients to be able to self-diagnose billing issues by simply looking at the balance in their Income accounts. If you usually have a balance of $20,000 in the account each Friday and on Thursday you see only $11,000 in the account, wouldn't it be much easier to notice an issue than it would be if that information was buried between payroll and rent payments?

OpEx: This account is for operational expenses like rent, software, dues, liability insurance, etc.

YOUR CURRENT CHECKING ACCOUNT SHOULD BECOME YOUR INCOME ACCOUNT TO AVOID ANY DELAYS IN PAYMENT.

Payroll: If you have employees or clinician contractors, you'll want to split payroll into its own bank account. Some practice owners try to run payroll within OpEx, but I don't recommend it. If you have a team, payroll will most likely be the largest expense in your business, and I want you to control the expense. A separate account will allow you to see the cash movements that are specific to payroll.

If you are the owner of an S or C corporation, you will cover your day-to-day personal expenses with both the paycheck you receive through payroll and a distribution through the Owner's Pay account (more on that account in just a moment). Payroll systems typically won't allow you to withdraw from two separate bank accounts, which is why your paycheck will be withdrawn from the Payroll account along with the rest of your team's paychecks and payroll taxes.

If you are a sole proprietor or own an LLC or partnership (that is not taxed as an S or C corporation) and you have employees, you will be paid through the Owner's Pay account, not the Payroll account.

If you are a solo practice owner with no employees and your business *is* taxed as a S corporation, you will need a PAYROLL account *or* an OWNER'S PAY account, not both.

If you are a solo practice owner with an administrative employee, you'll need both the PAYROLL and the OWNER'S PAY accounts.

OWNER'S PAY: This account is intended for your compensation and should ideally cover your day-to-day personal expenses.

If you are on payroll, this account will hold funds for your benefit, for regular distributions above and beyond your salary. You'll cover your day-to-day expenses with this account as well as the paycheck you receive from the PAYROLL account.

TAX: This account holds funds for the business to pay federal and state taxes on your behalf.

PROFIT: This account holds the profit intended for you, the owner.

Your current checking account will become your INCOME account. Your OpEx, OWNER'S PAY, and PAYROLL accounts should be business checking accounts, and you should get a debit card and/or checks for each. The PROFIT and TAX accounts should be business savings accounts.

Savings accounts give you a microscopic interest deposit each month, but they are much less flexible than checking accounts. Savings accounts typically have a transaction limit each month. After you reach the transaction limit, all other transactions will be blocked (check with your bank on your savings account transactions limit). While that *might* come in handy for the accounts you don't want to touch, it doesn't work for an account you need to access frequently, like PAYROLL.

To open the additional accounts, simply call your bank or go online to see if you can do it over the phone. In some cases, you'll have to physically go to the bank, but try a phone call and online banking first in case they save you a trip. When you've opened the accounts, give each of them a name or nickname in your online banking platform if possible. Your "old" checking account becomes INCOME, the new OPEX account gets a name as well, etc.

After you open these new accounts, get to work moving payments to them. If you run payroll, you know that connecting your payroll system to a new bank account can take a few days, so plan your timing accordingly. For example, if you pay your team every other Friday and payroll comes out of your account every other Wednesday, you can start changing the bank account on the Thursday morning after payroll funds have been withdrawn. This won't jeopardize your current payroll, but it will give you plenty of time to finish the setup before the next time you have to run payroll.

When Darla Sinclair, LCSW-C, owner of The Body Mind Center in Maryland, went to the bank to open new accounts, her banker thought it was ridiculous. Darla insisted and walked away with four new bank accounts. When she went back two years later to open more accounts, the same banker said she could see why Darla was doing what she was doing; she had accumulated a significant amount of money in the accounts since the date of their opening. So instead of making a snarky comment, the banker simply asked what names Darla wanted on the bank accounts without any pushback.

THERE ARE HUNDREDS OF ACCOUNTANTS AND BOOKKEEPERS AROUND THE WORLD WHO ARE CERTIFIED PROFIT FIRST PROFESSIONALS, BUT MAYBE *YOUR* ACCOUNTANT ISN'T ONE OF THEM. THEY MIGHT DISAGREE WITH YOU OPENING FIVE NEW BANK ACCOUNTS BECAUSE IT WILL CREATE MORE WORK FOR THEM. THE REALITY IS THAT PROFIT FIRST WILL ONLY ADD A HANDFUL OF NEW TRANSACTIONS EACH MONTH. I WOULD EVEN ARGUE THAT YOUR ACCOUNTANT'S JOB WILL BE EASIER WHEN YOU ARE ORGANIZED AND HAVE FUNDS SAVED FOR TAXES. YOU ARE THE BOSS OF YOUR BUSINESS, AND YOU GET TO DECIDE HOW TO RUN IT. FOR MORE INFORMATION ON WORKING WITH A PROFIT FIRST PROFESSIONAL, GO TO WWW.PROFITFIRSTFORTHERAPISTS.COM/TOOLS.

VAULT ACCOUNTS

MIKE MICHALOWICZ'S BOOK *PROFIT FIRST* recommends two additional accounts: the no-temptation vault accounts for PROFIT and TAX. These accounts are held at a separate bank, preferably one that is difficult to get to or withdraw funds from. In fact, Mike tells the story of his vault bank, a low-tech bank that does not have online access and requires a ninety-minute drive of shame in each direction. When Mike needs to withdraw funds from one of his two vault accounts, he's got to think long and hard to make sure it's worth the three-hour round trip.[4] Opening the vault accounts at a separate bank is a safety measure. It makes the accounts difficult to access, to ensure that the owner doesn't "accidentally" spend the funds on something else.

In my experience, therapists tend to be rule followers, and it's pretty rare for my team to see a client completely disregard the rules of Profit First and spend their payroll funds on, for example, a fancy new TV for their home. (In other industries, I absolutely *have* seen this. Years ago, I had a client who "accidentally" bought a fishing boat with the funds set aside for taxes.)

As an accountant, I've also seen firsthand how quickly a true financial emergency can happen: You were expecting a $10,000 deposit from Blue Cross Blue Shield on Friday (because you always get a BCBS check on Fridays) and this week, nothing. Payroll is due on Monday, and you simply don't have the option of not running payroll. It's already a very stressful situation, so not having to drive three hours to access your cash is a relief. Even if your vault bank allows ACH transfers, they typically take one or two business days to process.

In all the interviews I've done for this book, I can count on one hand the number of practice owners who have vault accounts at a different bank. Most practice owners don't use the vault accounts, and they have still been able to successfully implement Profit First. (I must also admit that I have used Profit First in my own business for years and have never opened vault accounts.)

For those reasons, I don't think that every practice owner needs vault accounts. Having your PROFIT and TAX accounts at the same bank as your INCOME, OPEX, and PAYROLL accounts can be helpful when you're in a real pinch.

That being said, you know yourself best. If you need the money to truly be out of sight, *do* open your vault accounts at a separate bank.

Ernesto Segismundo, who described his therapist guilt in Chapter 1, will be the first to admit that his relationship with money has been a rocky one. He has a deep love of casinos and shoes, and in his early days of implementing Profit First, he knew that if he saw a large amount of money just sitting in the PROFIT and TAX accounts, he'd be tempted to spend it.

To set himself up for success, Ernesto decided to add his sister as a cosigner to his PROFIT and TAX accounts. While he was still the owner, he couldn't withdraw funds without a second signature on the check. He was still able to make regular profit distributions and make his tax payments from the account, but he needed to get the signature of the cosigner to do so. That helped keep him accountable to his financial goals.

Ernesto also asked his bank to hide the accounts in his online banking portal. He knew that he was going to look at the account balances almost daily to see how much was available, and he truly wanted the funds to be out of sight and out of mind. As his relationship with money changed over the years, he eventually realized he was able to handle having full access. He no longer has a cosigner on his accounts, but he does have a VEGAS AND SHOES bank account because it allows him to spend whatever money is in that account without guilt.

If you feel like you might be tempted to spend your tax funds if they are at the same bank as your other accounts, I recommend using the vault accounts.

PRO TIPS

- I always suggest that your current checking account become your INCOME account instead of OpEx. It's a real pain to change where your insurance payments are deposited, and it's going to be much easier to move your bill payments to your new OpEx account instead of contacting each insurance carrier and making the change. It's not uncommon for a bank account change to delay your insurance deposits by two weeks or more, and some insurance companies will issue paper checks for an additional two weeks even though you've already set up ACH. Making the change can result in a few painful weeks, so just leave the deposits where they are. If you have a private-pay practice, you won't have that issue; simply change the bank with your payment processor, which typically takes two to three business days.
- When choosing a bank, make sure you're able to make a same-day transfer between accounts. Some tiny regional banks are very friendly and offer low fees, but do not have the capability to immediately transfer funds between two accounts at the same bank. When you're moving money, you should have access to it immediately.

TAKE ACTION: OPEN THE BANK ACCOUNTS

I KNOW YOU MIGHT BE thinking that you won't need the bank accounts, but you will. Whitney Owens, LPC, owner of Water's Edge Counseling in Georgia, went to open her accounts at a local bank fully expecting it to be a difficult and time-consuming process. She expected some pushback from the banker, so she had been putting off the task. It turned out to be very simple—to the point where she asked herself, *Why didn't I do that before?*

In some cases, opening the accounts can be a drag, as practice owner Colleen found out. She showed up at her small credit union's local branch excited to get started, only to find that the bank had no idea what Profit First was or why she would need that many accounts. Frustrated, she wanted to just hand them the book so they could get with the program. Colleen persisted and got her accounts open.

Angel said, "Opening all the bank accounts was obnoxious, but it was totally worth it. Just being able to have specific accounts, being able to mentally separate expenses and to think about my money that way, was so powerful for me. That's when the pieces finally clicked. It was even worth the bank fees."

As for me, I already had a checking and savings account at my credit union when I called to add more accounts. I was done adding two checking accounts and one savings account in under ten minutes. Easy!

If you're just getting started and are opening bank accounts for the first time, I highly recommend using a bank with a strong online banking portal. You'll be logging in often to make transfers, so this capability is an important one. If you need bank suggestions, head over to www.profitfirstfortherapists.com/tools.

CAN YOU STILL GROW YOUR BUSINESS IF
YOU TAKE YOUR PROFIT FIRST?

UNEQUIVOCALLY, YES.

BY TAKING YOUR PROFIT FIRST, YOU WILL TRAIN
YOUR BUSINESS TO BE PROFITABLE. THE FASTEST,
HEALTHIEST GROWTH COMES FROM PRACTICES
THAT MAKE PROFIT A PRIORITY. IT'S RARELY THE
ONLY PRIORITY, BUT IT'S ALWAYS *ONE* OF YOUR
PRIORITIES. TAKING YOUR PROFIT FIRST WILL FORCE
YOU TO REVERSE-ENGINEER YOUR EXPENSES.
YOUR PRACTICE, AND YOUR BANK ACCOUNTS, WILL
TELL YOU IMMEDIATELY IF YOU CAN AFFORD THE
EXPENSES IN YOUR BUSINESS OR ANY ADDITIONAL
EXPENSE YOU ARE CONSIDERING. IF YOU'RE UNABLE
TO PAY THE BILLS OR PAYMENTS BOUNCE,
YOU'LL NEED TO ADDRESS THE CORE ISSUES
WITHOUT ELIMINATING PROFIT.

THE FOUR CORE PRINCIPLES AT WORK

THE PROFIT FIRST SYSTEM USES your natural human tendencies to serve you better. Each account has its purpose and will help you achieve your goals. Let's recap the principles:

1. Use Small Plates – When money comes into the bank, it should go directly into your INCOME account. Each

account has its own objective, and this account will only have deposits, no debits.

2. **Serve Sequentially** – Allocate and transfer money to each of the accounts first, before paying the bills. You'll move money from the INCOME account into the OPEX (for operating expenses) and PAYROLL accounts; only then will you pay the bills. What if there isn't enough money left? This doesn't mean that you should borrow from the other accounts. This is your practice telling you, "I can't afford this!"

3. **Remove Temptation** – Move the money that shouldn't be touched out of reach immediately, into the TAX and PROFIT accounts. If you'll be tempted to borrow against these accounts, consider opening vault accounts at another bank.

4. **Enforce a Rhythm** – Allocate your funds at a regular cadence. After you get into the rhythm, you'll have a better grasp of the movement of cash in your business. There are several options for the frequency of your transfers: weekly, every other week, monthly, or on the tenth and twenty-fifth of each month. (Don't worry, we'll go over transfers in more detail in the next chapter.)

The first time I read Mike Michalowicz's *Profit First* as a new business owner and saw the principles laid out so clearly, I thought, *Of course, this makes so much sense! Why didn't I think of this?* I was so excited to jump in. I hope that's how you are feeling right now. This is the first of the Five Emotional Phases of Profit First, which I'll cover in detail in Chapter 6.

CHAPTER 3

Targets for Each Stage of Private Practice

WITH THE PROFIT FIRST SYSTEM, we use several bank accounts to trick ourselves into spending less, just as we might use small plates to eat less. Instead of using one bank account for everything, we split your funds into several accounts so you have a better sense of how much you can spend in each category.

When you have smaller amounts to work with, it might sometimes feel like there isn't quite enough for what you need or want. That's a normal part of the process, and it's what will help you get a little creative with how you cut your expenses or increase your revenue. That feeling of scarcity will help you make changes in your business.

Jacquie from my team had never seen anyone cut costs as ruthlessly as Giselle, a group practice owner in Georgia. When Giselle saw how high her expenses were compared to the industry averages Jacquie shared with her, she got serious about cutting overhead costs and streamlining her administrative processes to reduce overall spending. No stone was left unturned.

Because Giselle owns a private-pay practice, she knew that she would need to keep some funds allocated for advertising, but she reviewed all marketing expenses and kept only the ads that were generating results. When her administrative assistant left the practice, Giselle decided to get creative and make better use of the tools she already paid for so she wouldn't have to hire a replacement. She revamped their auto-receptionist system to handle the bulk of calls instead of having a live person answer the phone. Clinicians started taking payment at the time of service instead of having an admin handle that at the end of the day.

Another big expense was continuing education. Giselle is Gottman-certified and values having her team go through the certification process as well. She put procedures in place so that this made financial sense for the practice; clinicians on her team have to be employed with the practice for at least six months prior to starting the certification. They also have to stay with the practice for a minimum of one year or reimburse it for a portion of the training and certification expense.

With an eye on the bottom line, Giselle was able to slash her budget in a few short months.

Kasey Compton, M.Ed., LPCC-S, group practice coach and the owner of Mindsight Behavioral Group in Kentucky, is the Queen of Systems as far as I'm concerned. Her multimillion-dollar practice is very lean today, but it wasn't always that way. After intense growth in the first two years, her finances felt wobbly. As she implemented Profit First, Kasey decided that she would automate as many admin tasks as possible so her team could just manage systems instead of doing the work manually. Her practice can continue to expand without needing additional admin team members, which keeps her profit margin high.

After they had financial targets for various key business functions, both Giselle and Kasey successfully adjusted their spending.

ALLOCATIONS

YOUR FOUNDATIONAL BANK ACCOUNTS HAVE been set up, so now you may be wondering, *How much money should I transfer to each account?* That's where allocations come in. Each time you make a transfer, you will allocate a percentage of the funds in your INCOME account to your other bank accounts: PROFIT, TAX, OPEX, OWNER'S PAY, and PAYROLL.

Your goal will be the target allocation percentages, or TAPs. That's not necessarily where your practice is today, but it's where you are headed, the point on the map where you'll end up.

TARGET ALLOCATION PERCENTAGES (TAPs) → GOAL

I'd like for you to be able to visualize your destination, your target allocation percentages (TAPs), before figuring out where your practice stands today. My hope is that seeing the end result as if it's happened already will get you excited about the

Instant Assessment in the next chapter and encourage you to actually *do it.*

EXPENSE TARGETS FOR EACH STAGE OF PRIVATE PRACTICE

WHEN MY TEAM AND I started working with private practice owners, we noticed that what worked for large groups didn't work for smaller practices (and vice versa).

Now we constantly get the questions, "So, how are other practices in our situation doing? How much do they spend on xyz?" Years ago, we set out to "crack the code" of what a practice can reasonably expect to spend in various expense categories and generate in profit, in the form of target allocations or TAPs. They represent what's "normal" at each stage, and we know from experience that they are consistently doable. This isn't what the top 5% most profitable practices are doing; that would be discouraging for 95% of readers. These allocations have been tested consistently and I know they are achievable for you.

First, you need to know that I separate practices into four different sizes. What follows is a brief description of each, and you'll probably recognize your practice in one of them. Take note of the size that fits you best, and we'll use this to determine your target allocations (TAPs) in just a moment.

Solo Practice

Team: This one is self-explanatory. You, the owner, are the only person doing clinical work in your business. You may have an admin, biller, or virtual assistant (VA), but there are no other clinicians.

Revenue: A solo practice typically brings in $0–$250,000 each year, depending mostly on the number of sessions per week and the rate. $250,000 is mostly achievable in private-pay practices.

Characteristics: You, the owner, see all the clients and typically do most if not all of the work. The practice is like a canoe; you do all the paddling and go at your own speed. You can change directions as often and as quickly as you'd like.

Challenges: You wear many hats in the business, and that can be exhausting. If you don't want a group practice, the only ways to increase your revenue are to see more clients or raise your rate.

Small Group Practice

Team: Typically, a small group practice consists of two to four part-time clinicians, or maybe one or two full-time team members. There may be a part-time admin team member, or the owner might still be handling incoming calls, scheduling, and billing.

Revenue: Small group practices typically see annual revenue in the $150,000–$400,000 range, depending on whether the practice is private-pay or insurance-based and the number of clinicians.

Characteristics: In most cases, the owner is still seeing 50% or more of all sessions each week. For example, if the weekly session count is thirty-five and the owner sees twenty clients per week, the practice is considered a small group practice for the purposes of our target allocations. The practice is like a small motorboat; it can accelerate and slow down within seconds, and you have lots of control and can react quickly. But if a large storm comes along, you're likely to get wet.

Challenges: You're working really hard in this stage of practice, and not making much more money. You're likely seeing a full client load *and* doing most of the administrative work in the business, in part because it doesn't feel like you've got enough revenue to hire administrative help. In my opinion, this is the hardest stage of group practice. Because of that, some group practice owners decide to abandon ship and go back to solo practice.

Medium Group Practice

Team: There are typically five to eight clinicians on this team, depending on the mix of full- and part-time team members. One or more admin team members likely handle intake, billing, scheduling, and more.

Revenue: This practice brings in around $350,000–$1,000,000 annually, depending on whether the practice is private-pay or insurance-based and the number of clinicians.

Characteristics: The tipping point begins when more sessions are being done by non-owners in the practice. The owner sees less than 50% of sessions and, as the practice nears $1,000,000 in revenue, the percentage of sessions done by the owner decreases steadily. There are more systems in place and things generally start to feel less chaotic and a little easier. The practice is like a river cruise boat; it has a captain and a crew, and it's stable enough that you can sit down for dinner on it. Systems and processes are in place that make it possible to board dozens of passengers at the same time.

Challenges: There are a lot of people to manage in your practice at this stage, which can get heavy at times. It's almost impossible to know everything that is happening in the business because there's simply too much going on.

Large Group Practice

Team: A large group practice typically has at least eight to ten clinicians (again, depending on the mix of full- and part-timers). There are usually two or more people on the admin team who handle intake, billing, scheduling, recruiting, and more. One of the big changes at this size is the addition of leadership roles such as clinical director or site supervisor.

Revenue: Yearly revenue for a large group practice is somewhere in the $750,000–$5,000,000 range. We find that when a leadership level is added, there is no significant change to the target allocations as the business grows.

Characteristics: At this point, the owner typically sees fewer clients (if any) and their role is increasingly shifting toward big-picture or visionary work instead of day-to-day operations. Systems are in place that allow the owner to keep an eye on operations through metrics without having to be involved in each task. The practice is like a big cruise ship; it's stable and recognizable but can't turn around on a dime.

Challenges: By this point, owners have gotten used to delegating. If one of the delegates is no longer doing their work, it can take some time to notice that something is wrong. For example, I've had clients not realize that their biller had stopped resubmitting denials until they noticed that accounts receivable had ballooned to a record high. There is a significant amount of money flowing in and out of the business each month, so cash flow is more critical than ever.

Now that you have a better understanding of the characteristics of each practice size, let's dive into the recommended spending, which will be our target allocation percentages (TAPs). You'll notice that some of the percentages in Table 3.1 have a wide range. No two practices are exactly the same, so my goal is to give you a guideline instead of a rule. You'll have some flexibility to choose the target percentage that will work for you, as long as the total TAPs you select equal 100%.

Target Allocation Percentages (TAPs)				
	Solo	Small Group	Medium Group	Large Group
OpEx – Operating Expenses	10–40%	15–35%	10–25%	10–18%
Payroll – Therapists	0%	25–45%	45–60%	45–60%
Payroll – Admin	0–5%	0–5%	0–8%	4–7%
Payroll – Leadership	0%	0%	0%	3–5%
Payroll – Owner or Owner's Pay	30–60%	10–30%	5–10%	5–10%
Tax	5–35%	5–25%	5–15%	5–15%
Profit	5–15%	5–15%	5–10%	5–10%

Table 3.1: Target Allocation Percentages (TAPs)

OpEx – Operating Expenses: This is the amount you'll allocate for general overhead expenses such as rent, utilities, software, subscriptions, education, professional fees, advertising, office supplies, etc.

Payroll – Therapists: This is the amount you'll allocate for wages, payroll tax, and benefits for your clinician employees and contractors. This does not include the owner's wage if you are on payroll, even if you do clinical work.

Payroll – Admin: This is the amount you'll allocate for wages, payroll tax, and benefits for your admin employees and contractors.

Payroll – Leadership: This is the amount you'll allocate for wages, payroll tax, and benefits for your leadership team, like a clinical director, clinical supervisor, or site supervisor. The portion of their wage that is clinical should be allocated to *Payroll – Therapists*. For example, if your supervisor is salaried and does twenty clinical hours and ten supervisory hours each week, you'll allocate an amount that will cover one third of their wages in this section (10 supervisory hours/30 total hours).

Payroll – Owner or Owner's Pay: This allocation is intended to cover your personal living expenses. The logistics of how you pay yourself will depend on the tax entity of your business. If the owner is not on payroll, this is the amount you'll allocate for regular owner's draws to the owner. This amount will be available for a transfer to your personal bank account. If you are the owner of an S corporation or C corporation, this is the amount you'll allocate for your own wages, payroll tax, and benefits, as well as any regular distribution above and beyond your salary.

Tax: This is the percentage of revenue that your business will save to pay taxes, on your behalf.

Profit: This is the percentage that will be allocated for profit.

You'll notice that three of the allocations directly benefit you, the owner: *Payroll - Owner or Owner's Pay, Tax, and Profit*. They all benefit you directly or indirectly. The rest of the categories support your practice. All are important, and Profit First allows them to coexist in harmony.

TAX TAP: THERE IS NO ONE-SIZE-FITS-ALL TAX
CALCULATION BECAUSE EACH PERSON'S TAX
BURDEN CAN VARY SIGNIFICANTLY BASED ON
THEIR PERSONAL FINANCIAL SITUATION.
VARIOUS FACTORS WILL INFLUENCE THE
AMOUNT OF TAX YOU OWE EACH YEAR,
SUCH AS YOUR FILING STATUS (SINGLE, HEAD
OF HOUSEHOLD, OR MARRIED FILING
JOINTLY); YOUR DEPENDENTS; HOW MUCH
ADDITIONAL INCOME IS GENERATED IN YOUR
HOUSEHOLD; AND YOUR STATE TAX RATE. FOR
NOW, START WITH THE TAX TAP IN THE CHART,
BUT IT'S ALWAYS A GOOD IDEA TO CONSULT
WITH YOUR ACCOUNTANT OR TAX PREPARER TO
CONFIRM HOW MUCH YOU SHOULD BE SAVING.

FREQUENCY AND TIMING OF TRANSFERS

LET'S TALK ABOUT HOW OFTEN you'll make transfers. There
are four options available, and by the end of this chapter you'll
be ready to select the option that works best for your practice.
There is no right or wrong answer, and none of the following
cadences are "better" than any other. The options are:

- Weekly
- Biweekly (every other week)
- On the tenth and twenty-fifth of each month
- Monthly

If you have a team, one of the biggest drivers of your transfer frequency and timing should be your payroll. You'll always want to have enough money to pay your employees, so building your transfer timing to best suit your practice and its payroll schedule makes sense. More on that in just a moment.

If you don't have payroll, I find that the cadence of private practice deposits tends to lend itself better to biweekly (every other week) transfers, which is what I recommend most often. If you've read *Profit First,* you'll know that it recommends transferring funds on the tenth and twenty-fifth of each month. Although that can certainly work, those days will sometimes fall on weekends, when you might not be working. That means you'll need to remember to make your transfers on the previous business day or risk running out of funds in your accounts. Weekends tend to throw things off.

That's why I love biweekly transfers. I like the consistency of knowing that every other Friday, I make my own Profit First transfers. Always doing it on a Friday fits my schedule. It's the first thing I do after I get my kids off to school and log in for work. If it was sometimes on a Monday and other

CONSIDER HOW LONG THE TRANSFER PROCESS TAKES AS YOU DECIDE ON TRANSFER TIMING. IF YOU'RE TRANSFERRING BETWEEN ACCOUNTS AT ONE BANK, FUNDS WILL BE AVAILABLE IMMEDIATELY AND THERE SHOULDN'T BE A WAIT TIME. BUT IF YOU'RE TRANSFERRING FROM ONE BANK TO ANOTHER, IT COULD TAKE A FEW BUSINESS DAYS FOR THE FUNDS TO BE AVAILABLE.

months on a Wednesday, I'd have to fit my transfers in between all the other things I have scheduled on those days. Don't get me wrong: The transfers don't take much time at all, but I love having them as part of my Friday ritual.

If you're starting Profit First with a really tight cash flow, beginning with weekly transfers can also help you put buffers in place while still getting everything paid. After there are enough funds in each account for you to make it two weeks without making a transfer, you can switch to a biweekly schedule if you'd like.

One of our clients had tried to implement Profit First on her own and was struggling. When she started working with Kelly from my team, she was making transfers *daily*. At first, this brought her a sense of security. As soon as funds hit her INCOME account, she moved the money out right away. She was transferring to all four of her accounts each day in the hopes that she wouldn't run out of money, but there came a point where there were so many transfers, so much money moving in and out, that she got stressed out just thinking about it.

I am fully supportive of starting with weekly transfers. In fact, I think it can be very helpful while you get used to the process. Many of my firm's clients decide to stick with weekly transfers because they like the consistency and it forces them to do a quick check of their financial situation every week. It can allow you to really understand how money flows in and out of your practice. But daily transfers? Just say no.

After you choose a frequency and timing, stick with it for at least one or two months before you make any changes. It will take a few weeks to settle in.

PAY FREQUENCY MATTERS

IF YOU HAVE EMPLOYEES, YOU likely pay them based on one of these common schedules: once per month, twice per month, every other week, or every week. Depending on the state where your practice is located, there may be a specific *requirement* for how often you pay your team. (Check with an employment attorney.) If you pay your team every other week or every week, you will need to plan ahead for two to four months each year with additional pay dates.

What?

There are fifty-two weeks in one year. If your team is paid every other week, that means twenty-six pay periods in each year. Two months each year, you will have three pay dates instead of two. Your employees will love this, but for you: ouch. Those two months will have low or no profit, so you'll need to be prepared for a cash-flow crunch during those times.

If your team is paid every week, there will be fifty-two pay periods each year. Four months of each year, you will have five pay dates in one month instead of four. Ouch again.

If this is the situation you are in, you have two choices:

1. Choose a transfer schedule that mirrors your payroll schedule.
2. Build a buffer of cash throughout the year to cover the additional costs during these months.

Here are my transfer schedule recommendations based on the most common payroll schedules. Look up your own payroll schedule in the left column, and the right column will provide recommended transfer schedule options.

Payroll Frequency	Profit First Transfer Schedule Options
Monthly	Weekly Biweekly (every other week) On the tenth and twenty-fifth of each month Monthly
Bimonthly (for example, on the fifteenth and on the last day of the month)	Weekly On the tenth and twenty-fifth of each month
Biweekly (every other week)	Weekly Biweekly (every other week)
Weekly	Weekly Biweekly (every other week)

Table 3.2: Time Your Transfers Based on Payroll Frequency

One of the reasons I transfer funds every other Friday in my own business is that I run payroll every other Monday. This timing means I always make a transfer *before* I run payroll. I recommend that you do the same. After you select a transfer schedule, the transfers should occur a few days before you run payroll. Mark your calendar for your first transfer day!

TAKE ACTION: DETERMINE WHICH TAPs TO USE FOR YOUR PRACTICE AND YOUR TRANSFER FREQUENCY

CAN YOU PICTURE YOURSELF MAKING transfers with ease? Having enough funds in your accounts to pay for everything your practice needs? Good. There's a Chinese proverb that says, "The best time to plant a tree was twenty years ago. The second-best time is now." It doesn't matter how long you have been in business; you can't get that time back. You *can* take action now and transform your practice permanently.

Your action items for this chapter are simple:

1. Determine which target allocations (TAPs) you will use based on your practice size: solo, small group, medium group, or large group.
2. Decide how often you will make transfers: weekly, biweekly, twice per month on the tenth and twenty-fifth, or monthly.

CHAPTER 4

The Instant Assessment: Where Does Your Practice Stand Now?

NOW THAT WE HAVE SEEN your destination, let's figure out where your practice stands today by completing the Instant Assessment. It might feel a little scary, but I also know you're brave enough to face what's happening in your practice. I'll warn you that this is the driest chapter in the book, but I urge you to stay with me. Just as in the therapy room, we must push through the difficult parts to get to the good stuff.

When my mother first got sick, before she was willing to see a doctor and before she had a diagnosis, everyone in her life knew something was wrong—except her.

On our video calls, I could see her newly purchased walker sitting in a corner. I'd ask, "Mom, are you having a hard time walking?"

"No, honey, I'm fine," she'd reply. "My arthritis is flaring up, that's all."

When Mom started slurring her words, I'd have to close my eyes and concentrate to understand what she was saying during our calls.

I'd say, "I notice you are having a hard time speaking. Are you also having a hard time eating?"

"I'm fine," she'd reply. "I think I've got a little arthritis in my jaw, that's all."

When she finally saw a doctor, her situation had gotten so bad that she had to be rushed to the hospital from the exam room. By then, she could barely walk and hadn't eaten in four weeks. Because of ALS (also called Lou Gehrig's disease), the motor neurons that allowed her brain to control the muscles in her throat and left leg had deteriorated to the point where she was unable to swallow. Over the months, each day's change had been so small that she had convinced herself the situation wasn't getting worse at all. She anchored her beliefs in the facts she *wanted* to see, like the handful of days when there was a slight improvement. Her denial of the illness was so strong, she couldn't see that she'd lost significant mobility in just three months.

I know that you've encountered clients in a similar situation in your practice. Parents in denial of their children's struggles, spouses in denial of their partners' infidelity, people in denial of their own eating disorders. Because you've been in the therapy room with clients when they have their own lightbulb moments, you know that sometimes it takes a little nudge to help someone face reality. This is one of those times. You may be tempted to skip the Instant Assessment altogether because you'd rather not see—truly see—what's going on in your business. It might feel easier to stay in denial.

If you've come across this book because you're already stressed about money, you probably have a sense deep inside that something isn't right in your practice. You know that changes need to be made.

If your business is doing well but you know it could be even better, the Instant Assessment will help you fine-tune your financial systems. I encourage you to work through the exercise right now. Don't put it off. You'll get the most out of this book if you face your reality, good or bad, and stand in the truth of where your practice is today.

INSTANT ASSESSMENT

It's time to pull out a few reports:

1. Profit and loss* report (also referred to as a P&L or income statement)
2. Balance sheet*
3. Payroll reports

*Not sure what these reports are all about? I go over each in detail in Appendix 2: Making Sense of Your Financial Reports.

Use the longest period that is complete and accurate, ideally the last twelve months. This will help you catch variations and onetime expenses. If you only have a shorter period available, such as last month, last quarter, or the current year-to-date, use that.

If you don't have accounting records, pull out last month's bank and credit card statements and then add up the expenses (and income) in each category. This won't be perfect, but something is better than nothing and action is better than inaction. Once your documents are gathered, it should take between fifteen and sixty minutes for you to complete the Instant Assessment. The assessment will determine what your current allocations (CAPs) are, which is where your practice stands today.

TARGET ALLOCATION PERCENTAGES (TAPs) → GOAL

CURRENT ALLOCATION PERCENTAGES (CAPs) → WHERE YOU ARE TODAY

	Actual	CAPs	TAPs	PF$	The Bleed	The Fix
Real Revenue	A1					
OpEx – Operating Expenses	A2	B2	C2	D2	E2	F2
Payroll – Therapists	A3	B3	C3	D3	E3	F3
Payroll – Admin	A4	B4	C4	D4	E4	F4
Payroll – Leadership (if applicable)	A5	B5	C5	D5	E5	F5
Payroll – Owner (if applicable)	A6	B6	C6	D6	E6	F6
Owner's Pay (if applicable)	A7	B7	C7	D7	E7	F7
Tax	A8	B8	C8	D8	E8	F8
Profit	A9	B9	C9	D9	E9	F9
Totals	A10	B10	C10	D10	E10	F10

Table 4.1: Instant Assessment

YOU CAN DOWNLOAD AN ELECTRONIC COPY
OF THE INSTANT ASSESSMENT AT WWW.
PROFITFIRSTFORTHERAPISTS.COM/TOOLS. THIS
SPREADSHEET INCLUDES FORMULAS THAT WILL
RUN SOME OF THE CALCULATIONS FOR YOU. YOU'LL
ALSO FIND VIDEO RESOURCES FOR COMPLETING THE
INSTANT ASSESSMENT AT THIS LINK.

Let's start by completing the first column: Actual. I'll show you how to do so based on the following P&L and balance sheet examples. Note that the reports are for Q1, or three months, in a medium group practice.

Profit and Loss

January – March, 2023

	Total	
Income		
Therapy Income	103,380.00	
Total Income	**$ 103,380.00**	**Real Revenue**
Gross Profit	**$ 103,380.00**	
Expenses		
Operating and Overhead Expenses		
Advertising and Marketing	2,306.00	
Continuing Education	1,090.00	
Credit Card Processing	1,033.80	
Legal and Professional Services	1,270.00	
Office Software	826.00	
Office Supplies	1,872.00	
Telephone	728.00	
Total Operating and Overhead Expenses	**$ 9,125.80**	**OpEx**
Payroll Expenses		
Administrative Compensation		
Administrative Wages	7,480.00	
Administrative Payroll Tax	598.40	
Total Administrative Compensation	**$ 8,078.40**	**Payroll – Admin**
Officer Compensation		
Officer Wages	8,000.00	
Officer Payroll Tax	640.00	
Total Officer Compensation	**$ 8,640.00**	**Payroll – Owner**
Therapist Compensation		
Therapist Wages	55,927.00	
Therapist Health Insurance	790.00	
Therapist Payroll Tax	4,762.00	
Total Therapist Wages	**$ 61,479.00**	**Payroll – Therapists**
Total Payroll Expenses	**$ 78,197.40**	
Rent and Lease	2,700.00	**OpEx**
Total Expenses	**$ 90,023.20**	
Net Operating Income	**$ 13,356.80**	
Net Income	**$ 13,356.80**	

Balance Sheet

As of March 31, 2023

	Total
ASSETS	
Current Assets	
Bank Accounts	
Checking 1234	70,623.75
Savings 4321	18,354.00
Total Bank Accounts	**$ 88,977.75**
Other Current Assets	
Undeposited Funds	0.00
Total Other Current Assets	$ 0.00
Total Current Assets	**$ 88,977.75**
Fixed Assets	
Security Deposit	2,700.00
Leasehold Improvement	6,500.00
Total Fixed Assets	**$ 9,200.00**
TOTAL ASSETS	**$ 98,177.75**
LIABILITIES AND EQUITY	
Liabilities	
Current Liabilities	
Credit Cards	
Credit Card 0000	3,954.39
Total Credit Cards	**$ 3,954.39**
Total Current Liabilities	**$ 3,954.39**
Long-Term Liabilities	
Bank Loan	8,745.00
Total Long-Term Liabilities	**$ 8,745.00**
Total Liabilities	**$ 12,699.39**
Equity	
Additional Paid in Capital	20,000.00
Owner's Distribution	−9,000.00 Owner's Pay
Estimated Tax Payment	−1,000.00 Tax
Retained Earnings	62,121.56
Net Income	13,356.80
Total Equity	**$ 85,478.36**
TOTAL LIABILITIES AND EQUITY	**$ 98,177.75**

From your P&L, enter the dollar amounts for each category in the Actual column of the assessment.

A1: *Real Revenue* is the income generated by the practice. On the P&L, this appears as Total Income. If you don't have accounting records, add up the deposits for services in your business bank account.

	Actual
Real Revenue	103,380

A2: *OpEx – Operating Expenses* includes most overhead expenses that aren't payroll. My team and I like to nest operating expenses under an "Overhead" header directly in the accounting software for easy reporting. If your P&L isn't organized that way, just calculate the total operating and overhead expenses: rent, utilities, software, subscriptions, liability insurance, education, professional fees, advertising, office supplies, etc. This will include most non-payroll expenses. If you own the building your practice occupies, include the entire mortgage payment and all maintenance fees in this section. The following example shows the Total Operating and Overhead Expenses plus Rent and Lease.

	Actual
Real Revenue	103,380
OpEx – Operating Expenses	11,826

A3: *Payroll – Therapists* includes wages, payroll tax, and benefits for your therapist employees or contractors. If you are on payroll, do not include your wages here, even if you do clinical work. If all wages are displayed as one category like Payroll or Wages on your P&L, your payroll report will help you calculate this amount. You'll typically see an Employer Cost amount on the report that includes wages, payroll tax, and benefits. Add up the totals for all your clinical team members from your payroll report.

	Actual
Real Revenue	103,380
OpEx – Operating Expenses	11,826
Payroll – Therapists	61,479

A4: *Payroll – Admin* includes wages, payroll tax, and benefits for your admin employees or contractors. This includes outsourced virtual assistant services and billing contractors. If all wages are displayed as one category like Payroll or Wages on your P&L, your payroll report will help you calculate this amount. You'll typically see an Employer Cost amount that includes wages, payroll tax, and benefits on the report. Add up the totals for all your admin team members.

	Actual
Real Revenue	103,380
OpEx – Operating Expenses	11,826
Payroll – Therapists	61,479
Payroll – Admin	8,078

A5: *Payroll – Leadership* includes wages, payroll tax, and benefits for your leadership team. Allocate the portion of their pay for leadership time here. The portion of their wage that is clinical should be allocated to *Payroll – Therapists*. For example, if a supervisor spends 75% of their time doing clinical work and 25% of their time on supervisory duties, allocate 25% of their total cost to *Payroll – Leadership* and 75% to *Payroll – Therapists*. In this example, there is no leadership expense.

	Actual
Real Revenue	103,380
OpEx – Operating Expenses	11,826
Payroll – Therapists	61,479
Payroll – Admin	8,078
Payroll – Leadership (if applicable)	–

A6: *Payroll – Owner* includes wages, payroll tax, and benefits for the owner. This applies *only* if you are on payroll as the owner of an S corporation or C corporation. If you are not on payroll, enter 0. In the following example, the owner's wages, payroll tax, and benefits add up to $8,640.

	Actual
Real Revenue	103,380
OpEx – Operating Expenses	11,826
Payroll – Therapists	61,479

Payroll – Admin	8,078
Payroll – Leadership (if applicable)	–
Payroll – Owner (if applicable)	8,640

A7: If the owner is not on payroll, *Owner's Pay* will include the amount regularly paid to the owner. For example, if you pay yourself a $3,000 owner's draw each month (or $9,000/ quarter), enter it in this section. A distribution does not appear on the P&L, but you will find the year-to-date amount on the balance sheet.

If you are on payroll and pay yourself a regular distribution above and beyond your salary, include it here. In this example, the owner has received a distribution of $3,000/month (or $9,000/quarter).

	Actual
Real Revenue	103,380
OpEx – Operating Expenses	11,826
Payroll – Therapists	61,479
Payroll – Admin	8,078
Payroll – Leadership (if applicable)	–
Payroll – Owner (if applicable)	8,640
Owner's Pay (if applicable)	9,000

A8: If you currently save for taxes in the business or already pay your estimated tax from the business, include the amount here. If not, enter 0. This amount may appear as a separate line item on the balance sheet under the Equity section, or the tax payments may be hidden in an Owner's Draw or Distribution account with other personal transactions. In this example, the owner has saved $1,000 for taxes. For practice owners outside the United States, the way tax is reported on your P&L and balance sheet may differ from the following example.

	Actual
Real Revenue	103,380
OpEx – Operating Expenses	11,826
Payroll – Therapists	61,479
Payroll – Admin	8,078
Payroll – Leadership (if applicable)	–
Payroll – Owner (if applicable)	8,640
Owner's Pay (if applicable)	9,000
Tax	1,000

A9: To calculate your *Profit*, use the Net Income on the very last line of your P&L and subtract the amount in cell A8 for *Tax*. Your tax savings won't appear on the P&L, which is why we're subtracting it from your profit. Also subtract the amount in cell A7, *Owner's Pay*. For the following example, the calculation is Net Income – *Tax* – *Owner's Pay*, or $13,356.80 - $1,000 - $9,000 = $3,357 (rounded up).

	Actual
Real Revenue	103,380
OpEx – Operating Expenses	11,826
Payroll – Therapists	61,479
Payroll – Admin	8,078
Payroll – Leadership (if applicable)	–
Payroll – Owner (if applicable)	8,640
Owner's Pay (if applicable)	9,000
Tax	1,000
Profit	3,357
Totals	0

A10: After you've entered your numbers in the table, subtract rows A2 through A9 from A1. The total should be 0, or close to 0 because of rounding. If it's pretty far off, go back and check the numbers. If there's an issue, it's usually because of double-counting amounts between the *Owner's Pay, Tax,* or *Profit* categories.

Now that we have completed your Actual column, let's complete the rest of the Instant Assessment.

Step 1: Divide the actuals in column A by *Real Revenue* to get your CAP. Enter that amount in the CAPs column. For example, if your *Real Revenue* is $103,380 and your *Payroll – Admin* is $8,078, the CAP is 8,078/103,380 = 8%. Enter each percentage in the CAPs column. In this example, the practice currently spends 11% of its income on *OpEx*, 59% of its income on *Payroll – Therapists*, and 8% on *Payroll – Admin*.

	Actual	**CAPs**
Real Revenue	103,380	
OpEx – Operating Expenses	11,826	11%
Payroll – Therapists	61,479	59%
Payroll – Admin	8,078	8%

Step 2: In the TAPs column, enter the TAPs from Table 4.2 based on the size of your practice. In this example, I use the medium group TAPs and choose a TAP within the recommended range that makes sense based on the current spending in the practice. For example, if your current allocation percentage (CAP) for *Payroll – Therapists* is 59%, a realistic target allocation percentage (TAP) might be 55–57% if you think you might be able to hire interns or limit admin time. On the other hand, if your current allocation for *Payroll – Therapists* is 47% and you would like to add benefits for your team, you might choose a 50–51% TAP. After you have selected a TAP for each category, the total TAPs in cell C10 must equal 100%.

Target Allocation Percentages (TAPs)				
	Solo	Small Group	Medium Group	Large Group
OpEx – Operating Expenses	10–40%	15–35%	10–25%	10–18%
Payroll – Therapists	0%	25–45%	45–60%	45–60%
Payroll – Admin	0–5%	0–5%	0–8%	4–7%
Payroll – Leadership	0%	0%	0%	3–5%
Payroll – Owner or Owner's Pay	30–60%	10–30%	5–10%	5–10%
Tax	5–35%	5–25%	5–15%	5–15%
Profit	5–15%	5–15%	5–10%	5–10%

Table 4.2: Target Allocation Percentages (TAPs)

	Actual	CAPs	TAPs
Real Revenue	103,380		
OpEx – Operating Expenses	11,826	11%	12%
Payroll – Therapists	61,479	59%	60%
Payroll – Admin	8,078	8%	5%
Payroll – Leadership (if applicable)	–	0%	0%
Payroll – Owner (if applicable)	8,640	8%	5%
Owner's Pay (if applicable)	9,000	9%	5%
Tax	1,000	1%	7%
Profit	3,357	3%	6%
Totals	0	100%	100%

Step 3: The PF$ column shows the dollar amount you will allocate to each expense category after you have reached your target allocations. Calculate the PF$ by multiplying *Real Revenue* x TAP for each expense category. For example, if *Real Revenue* is

$103,380 and your *OpEx* TAP is 12%, then enter $12,406. The total in D10 should be equal to *Real Revenue*, the amount in A1.

	Actual	CAPs	TAPs	PF$
Real Revenue	103,380			
OpEx – Operating Expenses	11,826	11%	12%	12,406
Payroll – Therapists	61,479	59%	60%	62,028
Payroll – Admin	8,078	8%	5%	5,169
Payroll – Leadership (if applicable)	–	0%	0%	–
Payroll – Owner (if applicable)	8,640	8%	5%	5,169
Owner's Pay (if applicable)	9,000	9%	5%	5,169
Tax	1,000	1%	7%	7,237
Profit	3,357	3%	6%	6,203
Totals	0	100%	100%	103,380

Step 4: The Bleed is the difference between your PF$ numbers and actuals. In this column, you'll start with the amount in PF$ and subtract the amount in the Actual column. Remember, this is a no-judgment zone. Depending on where things fall, this number may be positive or negative, and that's okay. The total in E10 should always equal $0. If not, it's likely that the TAPs total is more than 100%.

	Actual	CAPs	TAPs	PF$	The Bleed
Real Revenue	103,380				
OpEx – Operating Expenses	11,826	11%	12%	12,406	580
Payroll – Therapists	61,479	59%	60%	62,028	549
Payroll – Admin	8,078	8%	5%	5,169	(2,909)

Payroll – Leadership (if applicable)	–	0%	0%	–	–
Payroll – Owner (if applicable)	8,640	8%	5%	5,169	(3,471)
Owner's Pay (if applicable)	9,000	9%	5%	5,169	(3,831)
Tax	1,000	1%	7%	7,237	6,237
Profit	3,357	3%	6%	6,203	2,846
Totals	0	100%	100%	103,380	0

Step 5: In the column titled The Fix, we'll simply indicate whether you need to increase or decrease spending.

	Actual	CAPs	TAPs	PF$	The Bleed	The Fix
Real Revenue	103,380					
OpEx – Operating Expenses	11,826	11%	12%	12,406	580	INCREASE
Payroll – Therapists	61,479	59%	60%	62,028	549	INCREASE
Payroll – Admin	8,078	8%	5%	5,169	(2,909)	DECREASE
Payroll – Leadership (if applicable)	–	0%	0%	–	–	NO CHANGE
Payroll – Owner (if applicable)	8,640	8%	5%	5,169	(3,471)	DECREASE
Owner's Pay (if applicable)	9,000	9%	5%	5,169	(3,831)	DECREASE
Tax	1,000	1%	7%	7,237	6,237	INCREASE
Profit	3,357	3%	6%	6,203	2,846	INCREASE
Totals	0	100%	100%	103,380	0	

Congratulations, you've made it through the Instant Assessment. If you're not sure how to complete your own Instant Assessment quite yet, I have many examples for you in just a moment.

START WITH 1%

IF YOUR CURRENT *PROFIT* OR *Tax* allocation is 0, you'll start with a CAP (your current allocation) of 1% for each. That's a total of 2% of your *Real Revenue*. You *can* run your business on 2% less, even if you have previously used every single dollar that your practice generates. If you can operate on $10,000 per month, I know you can find a way to run the practice with $9,800. If you can operate on $1,000 per month, you can do it with $980. And if you can operate on $100,000 per month, I truly believe that you can find a way to run the practice with $98,000. All I'm asking is for you to make a small, incremental change. There is a very good chance that 1% won't cover your entire tax bill. But if you've ever felt like you're playing catch-up at tax time because you haven't saved anything, can you imagine how good it will feel to have *something* to pay toward your taxes?

If you have already been saving much more for taxes, great job! Keep your allocation where it currently is or increase it by 1%.

EXAMPLES OF COMPLETED ASSESSMENTS

I just asked you to start with 1%, and you'll see that in action in the next table. Even though the *Tax* actual is $0 and the *Profit* actual is –$125, I still entered 1% in the CAPs column. That's because although nothing is currently being allocated to *Tax* or *Profit*, we will start with a 1% allocation for each on day one of Profit First implementation. That means we must reduce the other expense categories by 2% for the total allocations to equal 100%. In this case, I have reduced *Owner's Pay* by 1% and *OpEx* by 1%. We'll aim to get to TAPs of 7% for both *Profit* and *Tax* over time, as shown in the TAPs column.

	Actual	CAPs	TAPs	PF$	The Bleed	The Fix
Real Revenue	33,250					
OpEx – Operating Expenses	7,100	20%	19%	6,318	(783)	DECREASE
Payroll – Therapists	18,275	55%	40%	13,300	(4,975)	DECREASE
Payroll – Admin	–	0%	2%	665	665	INCREASE
Payroll – Leadership (if applicable)	–	0%	0%	–	–	NO CHANGE
Payroll – Owner (if applicable)	–	0%	0%	–	–	NO CHANGE
Owner's Pay (if applicable)	8,000	23%	25%	8,313	313	INCREASE
Tax	–	1%	7%	2,328	2,328	INCREASE
Profit	(125)	1%	7%	2,328	2,453	INCREASE
Totals	0	100%	100%	33,250	0	

Table 4.3: Small Group Practice with Negative Profit

In this example, it is likely that the owner is trying to dramatically reduce their caseload while keeping the same take-home pay. I suspect that the practice can't yet quite afford an owner who does not generate revenue. Because rent costs (within OpEx) are quite high, it's also possible that this practice is at the beginning of an expansion and needs to rapidly increase session counts. To sustain payroll costs at the high end of the recommended range based on the practice size, the owner will need to be very efficient with overhead expenses (OpEx).

	Actual	CAPs	TAPs	PF$	The Bleed	The Fix
Real Revenue	12,000					
OpEx – Operating Expenses	1,450	12%	12%	1,440	(10)	DECREASE
Payroll – Therapists	–	0%	0%	0	–	NO CHANGE
Payroll – Admin	–	0%	5%	600	600	INCREASE
Payroll – Leadership (if applicable)	–	0%	0%	0	–	NO CHANGE
Payroll – Owner (if applicable)	–	0%	0%	0	–	NO CHANGE
Owner's Pay (if applicable)	8,000	67%	65%	7,800	(200)	DECREASE
Tax	500	4%	9%	1,080	580	INCREASE
Profit	2,050	17%	9%	1,080	(970)	DECREASE
Totals	0	100%	100%	12,000	0	

Table 4.4: Solo Practice without Rent

These numbers show the story of a solo practice that is doing well and simply needs to allocate additional funds to *Tax* to avoid a tax surprise at the end of the year. We also see that there is opportunity to allocate funds to hire an admin or virtual assistant, which can enhance the quality of life of the practice owner and allow them more space for the work they do best.

	Actual	CAPs	TAPs	PF$	The Bleed	The Fix
Real Revenue	116,000					
OpEx – Operating Expenses	21,290	18%	15%	17,400	(3,890)	DECREASE
Payroll – Therapists	67,800	58%	56%	64,960	(2,840)	DECREASE
Payroll – Admin	4,800	4%	4%	4,640	(160)	DECREASE
Payroll – Leadership (if applicable)	6,700	6%	5%	5,800	(900)	DECREASE
Payroll – Owner (if applicable)	10,000	9%	10%	11,600	1,600	INCREASE
Owner's Pay (if applicable)	–	0%	0%	0	–	NO CHANGE
Tax	2,360	2%	5%	5,800	3,440	INCREASE
Profit	3,050	3%	5%	5,800	2,750	INCREASE
Totals	0	100%	100%	116,000	0	

Table 4.5: Large Group Practice with Leadership

These numbers show the story of a large group practice that is doing well but could use Profit First as an opportunity to rein in expenses. This could mean hiring interns or provisionally licensed clinicians at a lower rate to bring the *Payroll* allocation down slightly and capping leadership hours if the duties are hourly. While the rent paid won't decrease, increased efficiency in how the space is used would translate into higher revenue, decreasing the *OpEx* CAP (which includes rent).

After each Instant Assessment example, I have shared the story the numbers are telling us. After you complete your own Instant Assessment, I hope you'll see a story emerge as well. The numbers will show you which areas need adjustment. By looking at the big picture on paper, you can decide which expense category may need to go down or up.

If you've been drawn to this book at a point of financial stress, you may not feel ready to face the Instant Assessment. Because deep down, you know, right? You know this is going to be uncomfortable. Some people get downright mad after completing the assessment. Even for practice owners who think they are doing well, it can be a sobering experience.

Running the Instant Assessment is easy. Facing the truth about your business financials, on the other hand, is not.

Margo had just signed on to work with my team, and her monthly service package included Profit First implementation. After the kickoff call, her accountant, Carolyn, scheduled the Profit First implementation meeting where Margo, Carolyn, and my team would review the Instant Assessment and make a plan for the next twelve months.

The day of the meeting arrived and Carolyn waited in the video meeting room, ready to present the data. Five minutes, ten minutes, fifteen minutes went by. Carolyn called and emailed, but Margo was nowhere to be found.

The next day, we received a vague, apologetic email from Margo. No problem, things happen. The meeting was rescheduled for the following week.

Carolyn has a sunny personality, so on the next meeting day she sent a friendly reminder, probably with many exclamation points. She logged in to the meeting to find crickets again, so she sent another email and left another message. She didn't hear back for several days.

The meeting was rescheduled again, and Margo didn't show up for that one either.

"I don't get it," Carolyn said during one of our team meetings. "Why did Margo sign up to work with us if she doesn't actually want to see what we've done so far? Do you think she might not want to do Profit First after all?"

The truth is, sometimes clients ghost us. It typically happens when there's something big going on in their lives and they just don't have the emotional energy to deal with their finances. But this felt different.

Carolyn kept reaching out to Margo. She wanted to figure out what was going on. One day, surprisingly, Margo answered the phone. Carolyn took the opportunity. "Our team is worried about you, is everything okay?" she asked.

"I'm not sure," Margo said. "Actually, I've been avoiding you because I'm not sure I want to know what's really going on. I keep imagining the worst, and I just don't know if I can face it."

"What does the worst look like to you?" Carolyn asked. "Because in my experience, the worst-case scenario isn't usually *that* bad, and it's also pretty unlikely."

Margo thought for a moment, then responded. "I'm worried that I might have to shut down my practice. I just hired a few new clinicians, but they're not full yet and it feels like the business is hemorrhaging money. I'm not sure how I can get out of this hole. I don't want to work for someone else, but I also don't know how much longer I can do this. I'm exhausted."

Silence.

After a few moments, she continued. "Growing up, I never learned about money. I've never had a personal budget. I always figured that I'd have my financial life together by the time I was in my forties, but I haven't paid myself in weeks, and I won't be able to cover my personal expenses much longer."

"Well," Carolyn said, "I can't recall a single time I saw an Instant Assessment so bad that I told a client to immediately close their practice. You can scratch that off the list. But I do know that we can't make progress if you don't show up. You can't fix your business if you don't know what's happening. We just want to help. Do you think you're ready to take a look?"

She was.

Margo showed up to her meeting a few days later. Some tears were shed, but Margo faced her Instant Assessment. After Carolyn's presentation, Margo breathed a visible sigh of relief.

"When my kids were little, they were afraid of the monster in the closet," Margo said. "Each night, we'd go through the same routine. I'd read two books and tuck them in. Inevitably,

I'd get called to their room a few minutes later to check on the monster in the closet. I would turn on the light, open the doors wide, move the clothes and toys around, and show them there was no monster in the closet. Only then would they go to sleep. I feel like you just showed me that there isn't a monster in the closet."

It turns out that while Margo was in a tough period in her business, the Instant Assessment showed she wasn't *that* far from where she needed to be. Her practice income had increased, and so had her expenses. She would have to get serious about setting aside funds for taxes and a buffer for emergencies. Margo had been wanting to stop seeing clients but realized that wouldn't be possible until she stabilized the practice and got the expenses under control.

The Instant Assessment showed her that until her new clinicians filled their caseloads, she'd have to keep seeing clients herself. This wasn't what she wanted, but it's much easier to hang on when the end is in sight. She could also see that she needed to take a good hard look at her operating expenses and see what she could cut. She had a plan—and now that the lights were on and the closet doors were wide open, her situation wasn't scary anymore.

I'm happy to report that Margo stuck with Profit First beyond that first meeting and grew her team from three to twenty clinicians in just over two years. After nine months of stabilizing the business, she was able to decrease her caseload to ten clients per week. Now, two years later, she only sees five clients per week and only works with clients she truly enjoys.

TAKE ACTION: COMPLETE THE INSTANT ASSESSMENT

AFTER YOU'VE GATHERED ALL YOUR documents, this should take anywhere from fifteen to sixty minutes. Remember, establishing where your practice stands today is an important step toward taking your profit first.

Go to www.profitfirstfortherapists.com/tools to download the Instant Assessment. You'll also find video resources for completing the Instant Assessment at this link.

NEED HELP?

I KNOW THIS CHAPTER CONTAINS a huge amount of information. If you'd prefer to follow along with step-by-step instructions, I invite you to join my free, three-day Profit First Challenge.

Go to www.profitfirstfortherapists.com/challenge and you'll receive three daily emails to guide you through each section of the Instant Assessment.

CHAPTER 5

Time to Roll Up Your Sleeves: Implementing Profit First

Now that you know where your practice stands (CAPs) and where you are headed (TAPs), let's put it all together. In this chapter, I'll walk you through how to implement Profit First in your practice.

GETTING FROM YOUR CURRENT SITUATION TO YOUR TARGET (FROM CAPs TO TAPs)

When my team and I implement Profit First with our clients, we use a four- to eight-step process. During the first quarter, you make transfers based on your current allocation percentages, your CAPs. I know it can feel counterintuitive to stay exactly where you are, but you'll still see positive results. Depending on how much change needs to happen, it will take a few quarters of incremental changes to get from your CAPs to your target allocation percentages (TAPs). If you'd like the change to happen more quickly, I still recommend four to eight steps, but with monthly changes instead of quarterly ones. That will give your practice time to adapt in between and, if needed, you can hold for an additional month before moving on to the next step.

Table 5.1 shows a four-quarter rollout over one year. Each quarter, the expense categories either go up or down by a small percentage, depending on the "fix" shown in column F of the Instant Assessment. The amount in The Fix column is divided by three to calculate the Q2-Q4 CAPs for a four-quarter rollout, or divided by seven to calculate the Q2-Q8 CAPs for an 8-quarter rollout. Over time, the *OpEx* allocation goes from 23% to 15%—that's an 8% swing. You can imagine how challenging it would be to do that in one or two months. Instead, the four-quarter rollout reduces the *OpEx* allocation by 2–3% each quarter (depending on rounding) to give the practice time to adjust and make changes each quarter.

Phase 1: Year 1							
	CAPs	**Q1**	**Q2**	**Q3**	**Q4**	**TAPs**	**The Fix**
OpEx – Operating Expenses	23%	23%	20%	18%	15%	15%	-8%
Payroll – Therapists	63%	63%	61%	58%	56%	56%	-7%
Payroll – Admin	5%	5%	5%	5%	5%	5%	0%
Payroll – Leadership (if applicable)	2%	2%	3%	3%	4%	4%	2%
Payroll – Owner (if applicable)	5%	5%	7%	8%	10%	10%	5%
Owner's Pay (if applicable)	0%	0%	0%	0%	0%	0%	0%
Tax	1%	1%	2%	4%	5%	5%	4%
Profit	1%	1%	2%	4%	5%	5%	4%
	100%	100%	100%	100%	100%	100%	0%

Table 5.1: CAPs to TAPs Rollout

Pssst: The Instant Assessment at www.profitfirstfortherapists. com/tools will automatically calculate your four or eight-period CAPs to TAPs.

LOWER THE BAR

I WANT YOU TO REMEMBER that your TAPs are *not* the starting point; they are your destination. As a business owner, you're probably an overachiever, and I know you might be tempted to start with allocations that are significantly different than your CAPs. Don't do it.

In this process, you'll be intentional about paying yourself and taking your profit first, but your business still needs to survive. By moving too quickly, you risk depriving your business of the resource it needs most: cash. Start where you are today and slowly work your way up to the goal percentages (TAPs) you just identified.

Kate Fish, LMFT, PMH-C, owner of Graceful Therapy in Illinois, couldn't understand why we weren't starting with TAPs when my team walked her through the first stage of Profit First implementation. "If we know the TAPs are where my practice needs to be, why wouldn't we start there?" she said. "If my CAPs are all wrong, why are we going to stay there even one more day?"

We asked Kate to trust the process, with the promise that if she was on track, we'd reevaluate the allocations in one month instead of waiting a full quarter. As the weeks and months went by, it became clear that smaller steps were the key to her success. She made small changes to her allocations, sometimes half a percentage point, and kept going. Each time, she had to reevaluate her spending and find efficiencies before the dust fully settled. That's when Kate realized that it would have been almost impossible to go from a 0% to a 10% *Profit* allocation right away—and that it would have been so discouraging to fail so soon.

A few months later, Kate shared, "Now I understand that my business needed to change gradually, not all at once. I needed that time to make it work. Now I get why I needed to start where I was to be successful."

Just like Kate, you'll start where you are today with a few small tweaks and make incremental changes every few months. That will give you time to make small adjustments in your practice each week or each month instead of having to blow up your spending and change everything on day one.

I fully support you setting stretch goals for your TAPs, something that will challenge you. Playing it safe isn't all that helpful when it comes to goals, especially if it allows a halfhearted effort. But that doesn't mean we can skip to the end; we need to map out the journey. The most common reason I see for practice owners giving up on Profit First is that they tried to go too fast and skip to the end. If Profit First is a race, be the tortoise, not the hare.

THE WRONG WAY TO SET UP PROFIT FIRST

I OFTEN ENCOUNTER PRACTICE OWNERS who want to subtract all payroll from *Revenue* to calculate *Real Revenue,* and then calculate CAPs on the remaining amount only. Setting up Profit First this way does not address the single largest expense in the business: payroll. For that reason, I don't recommend this method.

I understand why it can be so tempting to do, though. After all, the formula from the original *Profit First* book *does* tell you to subtract "Materials and Subcontractors" from your *Revenue* to get to *Real Revenue*. That's because it assumes that you won't have any control over the costs of "Mats and Subs," like a construction company that must buy lumber at market rate.[5] If you don't have control, materials shouldn't factor into your CAPs calculations.

In private practice, though, you do have control over clinician compensation, whether you have employees or contractors. You are the one who negotiates the contract and sets the rate, agrees to a raise, or decides to add benefits. Because you have control, I recommend that you include payroll in your allocations.

Every time I share this opinion with someone who is currently running Profit First this way, I get a groan. "Julie, I have to make sure there is enough money for payroll, I can't just *not* pay my employees." True. However, when you subtract payroll from revenue before calculating allocations, you won't hear the alarm bell alerting you that something is wrong—or you won't hear it nearly as fast.

My client Kristen's PAYROLL account acts a barometer for the business. She has a few salaried admin and leadership positions, and her clinicians are paid a percentage of the revenue they generate. Because the clinicians get paid when funds are received by the business, there is always enough money to cover their payroll. But a dip in income can mean that paying administrative and leadership salaries from the same account gets tight. When that happens, it immediately sends her team into problem-identifying mode: Are session counts down? Are intakes down? Do we have higher accounts receivable than usual?

If Kristen subtracted payroll before calculating her CAPs, it would likely take her weeks longer to start looking for a bottleneck.

MAKING THE FIRST TRANSFERS

In Chapter 3, we reviewed the various options for transfer timing. If you haven't already, it's time to decide which option you want to use: weekly, biweekly, bimonthly on the tenth and twenty-fifth, or monthly. Add a reminder to your calendar now. To determine how much money to transfer to each account, use the Transfer Calculator in Table 5.2. In the CAPs column, enter your current allocations for each line item. Each quarter, you'll change the allocations. Then, in the Income Bank Balance row, enter the bank balance of your Income account on the day of your transfer. Next, you'll calculate the amount to transfer by multiplying the Income Bank Balance by each allocation and entering that amount in the *Transfers* column.

	CAPs	Transfers
INCOME Bank Balance		
OpEx – Operating Expenses		
Payroll – Therapists		
Payroll – Admin		
Payroll – Leadership (if applicable)		
Payroll – Owner (if applicable)		
Total Payroll		
Owner's Pay (if applicable)		
Tax		
Profit		
	100%	

Table 5.2: Transfer Calculator

Go to www.profitfirstfortherapists.com/tools to download the Transfer Calculator.

One key step in setting yourself up for success is to make sure each account has enough funds to cover expenses until the next transfer day. That usually means that the balance of your checking account (now your INCOME account) will need to be split based on your CAPs and transferred to each account. Let's say there is a balance of $50,000 in your checking account; you will fund the other bank accounts as shown in Table 5.3. Your initial transfers will include $9,500 to OpEx; $39,500 to PAYROLL, which we calculate by adding the totals in *Payroll – Therapists, Payroll – Admin, Payroll – Leadership*, and *Payroll – Owner*; $500 to TAX; and $500 to PROFIT.

	CAPs	Transfers
INCOME Bank Balance		50,000
OpEx – Operating Expenses	19%	9,500
Payroll – Therapists	60%	30,000
Payroll – Admin	4%	2,000
Payroll – Leadership (if applicable)	6%	3,000
Payroll – Owner (if applicable)	9%	4,500
Total Payroll		39,500
Owner's Pay (if applicable)	0%	0
Tax	1%	500
Profit	1%	500
	100%	50,000

Table 5.3: First Transfers

Here is what your online bank portal might look like prior to the first transfer:

No Name Bank

Business Accounts

Business Checking – 0000	$ 50,000.00

After the initial transfers, your online bank portal will look like the following image. It's the same amount of money, but Profit First makes it incredibly easy to see how much money is allocated to each expense category.

No Name Bank

Business Accounts

Business Checking – OPEX – 0001	$ 9,500.00
Business Checking – PAYROLL – 0002	$ 39,500.00
Business Checking – INCOME – 0000	$ –
Business Checking – PROFIT – 0003	$ 500.00
Business Checking – TAX – 0004	$ 500.00

On the next transfer date, calculate your transfers based on your current allocations (CAPs) and the balance in your INCOME account and transfer funds to each of your bank accounts: OPEX, PAYROLL, OWNER'S PAY, TAX, and PROFIT. You'll use the same Transfer Calculator, and once again you'll enter the balance of your INCOME account in the INCOME Bank Balance row, and then multiply each CAP by that amount. In the example in Table 5.4, the balance in the INCOME account on the transfer day is $18,945. Because the *OpEx* allocation is 19%, $3,600 will be transferred to the OPEX account (19% x $18,945 = $3,600).

	CAPs	Transfers
INCOME Bank Balance		18,945
OpEx – Operating Expenses	19%	3,600
Payroll – Therapists	60%	11,367
Payroll – Admin	4%	758
Payroll – Leadership (if applicable)	6%	1,137
Payroll – Owner (if applicable)	9%	1,705
Total Payroll		14,967
Owner's Pay (if applicable)	0%	–
Tax	1%	189
Profit	1%	189
	100%	18,945

Table 5.4: Completed Transfer Calculator

PROFIT FIRST PROCESS SUMMARY

NOW THAT WE HAVE REVIEWED the basics of Profit First, here is a recap of the setup and ongoing maintenance of your Profit First System.

Profit First setup:

1. Open three business checking accounts using your current bank. Ask for checks and a debit card for each if needed.
   a. OPEX
   b. PAYROLL (if needed)
   c. OWNER'S PAY
2. Open two business savings accounts.
   a. PROFIT

    b. TAX

3. Your existing business checking account becomes your INCOME account.
4. Determine which target allocations (TAPs) you will use (Appendix 4).
5. Complete the Instant Assessment (Appendix 5).
6. Decide on a transfer frequency (weekly, biweekly, twice monthly on the tenth and twenty-fifth, or monthly).
7. Make your initial transfers with the Transfer Calculator (Appendix 6).

Each transfer day (weekly, biweekly, twice monthly on the tenth and twenty-fifth, or monthly):

1. Transfer funds from your INCOME account to the PROFIT, TAX, PAYROLL, OWNER'S PAY, and OPEX accounts based on your CAPs. Combine all the *Payroll* line items into one transfer.
2. Look at the balance of each account to make sure there are enough funds for the expected expenses. If not, consider deferring an expense or do some troubleshooting to find out why there isn't enough money in the account.
3. Trust the process.

Quarterly:

1. Pay your estimated tax payment or the amount due with your tax return from your TAX account. (If there is any money left, leave it!)

2. Take half of the balance in your PROFIT account for your-self. Leave the other half in the account as an emergency fund.
3. Review the CAPs to TAPs worksheet and adjust your current allocations (CAPs) to the next quarterly step toward your target allocations (TAPs).
4. Trust the process.

You can find a downloadable copy of this Process Summary at www.profitfirstfortherapists.com/tools.

BUFFERS

DEPENDING ON HOW MUCH INCOME you generate between transfer days, you may find that you have more money than you need in some of your accounts. If this is the case, you might be tempted to transfer less. Don't.

Building a buffer into each account is one of the best things you can do. Think about your practice and the natural seasonality of the work you do. For example, our clients who work mostly with children know the summer is usually slower and they will be slammed in September when school starts again. When you build up buffers during the "good" months, they will sustain you through the "slow" months. Occasionally a slow month can come as a surprise, perhaps because of a billing issue. Taking only what you need and letting your bank balance grow builds a small emergency fund right into your practice.

OWNER'S PAY

IN AN IDEAL WORLD, THE amount you transfer to the OWNER'S PAY account is enough to support your personal lifestyle. If you're unsure how much you need to take home, we'll discuss it in more detail in Chapter 9. We'll look at your ideal lifestyle and reverse-engineer your practice to provide for you.

Depending on how much income you generate between transfer days, you may find that you have more money than you need in the OWNER'S PAY account. You should take the amount you need and leave the rest for a rainy day. The goal of this account is to take care of *you*, so the buffer will help offset the weeks when there isn't quite enough to cover your minimum take-home pay.

PAYROLL

YOUR TRANSFER TO THE PAYROLL account will likely be the largest one you make. In the TAPs and the Instant Assessment, I show separate line items for therapists, admin, leadership, and owner payroll. I like to see each item separately because it helps practice owners keep an eye on the various departments included in payroll. When it comes to actually making transfers, though, you'll combine all four line items into one transfer from the INCOME account to the PAYROLL account.

PROFIT

ONE OF THE MOST REWARDING parts of Profit First is watching the balance of the PROFIT account grow. These funds will be part savings and part reward. Quarterly, you'll take half of the balance in your PROFIT account for yourself. This is your reward for being a shareholder in your business. It's time to celebrate!

Some of our clients create a fun ritual around the profit distribution, like treating their family to a meal at a fancy restaurant. Another client used the funds to purchase something her family has wanted for a long time: a hot tub. Other clients have used their profit distributions to pay down student loans and plan family trips to destinations they had never been able to afford in the past. A quarterly distribution is an important milestone worth celebrating.

After you have distributed half of the balance in the PROFIT account to yourself, the other half of the funds will stay in the business as a buffer or additional savings account. I know it might be tempting to borrow from your PROFIT account when you need a little cash, but I only recommend this in extreme circumstances.

If you have significant debt, you may want to use some of these funds to pay down your loan balances. We'll talk more about this in Chapter 12.

TAX

DEPENDING ON WHERE YOU ARE in your Profit First journey, it's possible that the amount in your TAX account either A., won't cover your full tax liability, or B., will be more money than you think you need. If you're in situation A, you'll want to increase your *Tax* allocation as quickly as possible before you increase your *Profit* allocation. Taxes will be due no matter what, and I'd rather you have enough money in the Tax account than have to borrow from Profit or worse, not pay your tax balance.

If you're in situation B, leave the funds in the Tax account until *after* your personal tax return has been filed. Even if you paid your quarterly estimated tax payments in full, you may still have a balance due at the end of the year. Also, in the US, your year-end tax liability and first quarter estimated tax payment are both due on April 15. This tends to take some business owners by surprise, even though it's the case every year.

STARTUP PRACTICE

Can Profit First still work if you're just starting out? Absolutely! After your initial investment, you can implement Profit First as early as the first dollar generated by the practice.

You typically need to invest some personal funds to get your practice off the ground. Whether it's $500 or $5,000, you decide what makes sense for you based on your personal situation. Make a plan for these funds, including how quickly you will start to generate income. This entire initial investment will go to OpEx, not the Profit, Tax, or Owner's Pay accounts. That's because your initial investment is not revenue and is not taxable.

Because you won't have CAPs, you can start immediately with the solo practice TAPs and adjust as needed afterward.

This will help guide your spending and allow you to start off on the right foot. It will ensure that your business has the financial resources it needs, and that you'll get paid from the very first session.

PRO TIPS

THERE ARE LOTS OF PRACTICAL tips I've learned that are specific to private practice, so I want to share them with you as well.

- If your bank requires a minimum balance to avoid fees, leave that amount in your INCOME account each time you transfer. For example, if your bank requires a minimum of $500 in your account and your INCOME balance is $4,500, calculate your transfers based on $4,000.
- I highly recommend building a buffer into each account, especially if your practice accepts insurance. Payment issues tend to come up more often for insurance-based practices, so having extra money in each account (except PROFIT) for emergencies will help you if insurance stops paying.
- As you get started, I want you to look at how much you *know* you'll need in an account until the next transfer. If your initial transfer isn't at least that amount, you are setting yourself up for failure. For example, if your $2,500 rent is due next week but you're only transferring $1,700 to OPEX, you simply won't be able to wait two weeks until

your next transfer. You must be realistic, or you'll panic midweek and start moving money around. That doesn't help. If you're starting Profit First with some extra cash in the bank, pad your accounts a little. My goal is for you to eventually see a one-month reserve in each account.

- If you're really stressed out about the idea of having to pay non-sufficient funds (NSF) fees on your account, consider setting up overdraft protection with your bank. Full transparency: I don't love overdraft protection because it can sometimes be a security blanket, but if it removes a barrier to implementation, it might be a good solution for you. Your ultimate goal is to fund all the accounts properly, but if you missed the mark somewhere, this can be a good fail-safe.

You might be a little skeptical at this point. It's normal. It's easy to come up with a lot of reasons to give up before you even start. My team and I have worked on over a hundred Profit First implementations, and the Profit First community has implemented the system thousands of times. Trust the process. It really does work.

We'll cover the common questions and mistakes shortly, in Chapter 7. We'll also explore complex situations in Chapter 8.

I am often asked how long it takes to see results with Profit First. The answer truly depends on you. Now that you know where your practice stands, are you willing to make changes right away—like opening the bank accounts and reducing your expenses—to accelerate toward your target allocations? If the answer is yes, you'll see results quickly.

TAKE ACTION: GETTING STARTED CHECKLIST

DID YOU SKIP ANY STEPS when setting up Profit First? If so, refer to the Getting Started Checklist in Appendix 7 to complete your Profit First setup.

CHAPTER 6

The Emotional Journey of Profit First

AFTER IMPLEMENTING PROFIT FIRST OVER and over within the mental health industry, I've noticed that practice owners often go through similar emotional journeys during the process. Most of them experience the Five Emotional Phases of Profit First. The journey is not linear, and not everyone will experience each phase. In an earlier draft of this book, I compared the phases to the Kübler-Ross Grief Cycle. I probably don't need to remind you, but the five stages of that model are denial and isolation, anger, bargaining, depression, and acceptance. An early reader was kind enough to share that the five stages of grief have received much criticism over the years and have been revised, so I now realize the comparison isn't quite accurate.

The Five Emotional Phases of Profit First look like this:

1. Excitement
2. Resistance
3. Overwhelm
4. Aha!
5. Acceptance and Delight

Profit First is a simple framework for financial freedom that works incredibly well. Every practice owner's implementation experience will be unique, and there is a chance the road to success for you won't be completely linear, smooth, or lined with rainbows and unicorns. I also know you might be feeling a little overwhelmed after the Instant Assessment. That is so normal.

The Five Emotional Phases of Profit First is a tool to help you identify what you are going through if the going gets tough. I hope it will help you validate the emotions you are feeling and push through to the Acceptance and Delight phase. Let's explore each phase.

EXCITEMENT: I'M READY TO MAKE A CHANGE—LET'S DO THIS!

It's easy to get excited about implementing Profit First after reading this book. I hope you are pumped and ready to go all in. You understand how the system will work, and you are going to *crush it*. You're going to take your profit first, and you can almost taste the fancy dinner you'll reward yourself with at the end of the first quarter.

If you're at the Excitement stage, strike while the iron is hot. Gather your business paperwork and run to the bank to open those accounts if you haven't done so already. Grab your P&L and get started on the Instant Assessment if you skipped it in Chapter 4. Movement is key, so take advantage of the excitement to get things done. You've got this!

It's a great idea to enlist an accountability partner or reach out to a Profit First Professional (PFP) while you're still excited about the process. You might not feel like you need support yet, but that could change down the line and it's helpful to have someone to turn to when you do. You'll want your accountability partner to have a basic understanding of Profit First and be committed to creating a judgment-free space for you to talk through your challenges. Go to www.profitfirstfortherapists.com/tools for resources and tips on finding an accountability partner or PFP.

I see this phase with most clients who work through implementation with us. In the first few weeks, our clients are walking on clouds, excited to see how the system will change their lives. They practically skip to the bank to open their accounts.

RESISTANCE: I'LL DO IT MY WAY—JUST GIVE ME THE PERCENTAGES

You've completed the Instant Assessment and you may be a little bummed out. Perhaps your business isn't doing quite as well as you had hoped, and you just realized there's a long way to go to get where you'd like to be. So even though I recommended that you start with *Profit* and *Tax* allocations of 1%, you start with 5% each because that will get you to your goal faster. Then you bounce a payment. You have enough money in the bank; it just wasn't in the right account. (Seriously, this happens to 99% of people who implement Profit First at some point. Including me. Years ago, my own team payroll bounced because I forgot to make a transfer to the PAYROLL account. Oops!)

Then you begin to "borrow" from the other accounts to cover expenses, and Profit First seems like a tangled mess that isn't quite worth it. You start to consider just using a separate Excel spreadsheet to track the theoretical amounts in each account instead of using the actual bank accounts.

If you're at the Resistance stage, don't give up. Stick with it—you *can* do it. Go back to 1% *Profit* and *Tax* allocations and take it slow. This is a lifestyle change, not a fad diet. These things take time and there will be setbacks.

My client Alaina really wanted to implement Profit First, but she wanted to do it *her* way. We'd calculate her biweekly transfers and share the amounts with her, but she almost never transferred based on the allocations. She'd raise or reduce them each period depending on what she felt like buying and was constantly borrowing from the PROFIT account. At one point, I had to have a heart-to-heart with her because I didn't want to continue down this half-paved road. As we chatted on Zoom one afternoon, I asked her what she thought about Profit First.

"I just don't know, Julie. It doesn't seem like this is working."

"I agree," I said. Her jaw dropped. This wasn't the response she was expecting from me. "What you're doing isn't Profit First, Alaina. You try to transfer way too much to PROFIT, then as soon as you're short, you transfer the money right back to your PAYROLL or OPEX account. On top of that, you haven't reduced your expenses, so how could this possibly work?"

Here's the thing: Profit First is not a magic wand that will immediately make your practice more profitable. The system works incredibly well, but it requires you to make *some* changes and do the work. It will give you better awareness of your finances, but you must act to get the results.

My accounting firm implements Profit First in dozens of private practices each year. Even though our clients are supported every step of the way, they can still go through the Resistance phase, especially when money is really tight. It's easy to implement Profit First when you're swimming in piles of cash. When you're struggling? That's when it's tricky. It can also be painful to truly look at where you have been spending your money. There's no need for a shame spiral here, though. Your money isn't judging you.

If you're implementing Profit First on your own, this is the time to lean on your accountability partner. It's normal to doubt yourself at this phase, and I hope that knowing this is par for the course can help you believe it will get easier. Thousands of business owners have gone through the implementation process and come out the other side with businesses that are more profitable.

OVERWHELM: WHAT IS HAPPENING?!

AT THIS STAGE, THINGS ARE kind of working but Profit First still feels like a chore. You are annoyed at having to make the transfers even though you're seeing some positive movement. You might even be questioning whether this Profit First thing can transform your business.

This stage can also feel like you've lost control or taken a step back. Whitney Owens, who shared her experience opening Profit First bank accounts in Chapter 3, had to *reduce* her *Owner's Pay* allocation when she implemented Profit First recently, in part because a portion was needed for *Profit, Tax,* and *Payroll.* In the long run, though, Whitney will earn more money; and a few months later, she's already seeing the upside of the allocations, like being able to add benefits for her team. But "down the road" benefits don't make the moment of reducing your take-home pay any less scary.

It's possible that you could end up in the Overwhelm phase multiple times, even after your Profit First journey has been bumping along without many issues. A time of crisis or an unexpected event could throw you a curveball.

I remember vividly one January a few years ago when we had several insurance-based clients struggling with cash flow. January is typically a lower-revenue month for most practices, just because session counts tend to slow down in December. Clients are on vacation or skip their appointments during the holidays, and you and your team might take time off as well. We expect a financial lull in January, a few weeks after the session lull. That January, though, it seemed like insurance companies just stopped making payments. Almost every single one of our insurance-based clients saw a big dip in deposits. All but the most prepared of practices struggled. If payroll is due and you are short thousands in insurance payments, you're going to feel overwhelmed.

If you're at this stage, trust that it is temporary. Sometimes just knowing that things are going to be a little painful but the pain is temporary is enough to get you through, isn't it? That's why I'm sharing this with you. Overwhelm is a normal part of the process that will eventually end. These difficult moments will happen whether you implement Profit First or not, so they don't mean that the system is failing.

Keep in mind that it may also take several iterations to get the allocations "just right." That's okay. Better to keep trying until you get it right than to give up.

Dr. David Goode-Cross, MA, PhD, owner of East Towson Psychological Services in Maryland, had several moments of frustration with Profit First, most of them due to the PAYROLL account not having enough funds to pay his team. He had tried to start the allocation as low as possible, at 50%. It didn't work. He kept iterating, increasing the allocation by a few percentage points each time. When he finally tried a 70% allocation, everything clicked. "It was just smooth sailing from that point. I had been trying to keep more funds in OpEx because I thought that's where they should be, but the truth is, I don't have a lot of expenses. I needed the funds in PAYROLL because it covers my clinical and admin team's wages as well as my salary. When I finally understood that, it changed everything. The frustration was gone," David told me.

One day, you'll wake up and feel pretty good about Profit First. That's when you'll know you've exited the Overwhelm stage. If you'd like to get there faster, check out www. profitfirstfortherapists.com/tools to find resources like the Profit First for Therapists Facebook group, tips to find the right accountant for you, and more.

AHA! I HAVE MONEY TO PAY MY BILLS—AND MYSELF!

GETTING TO THE AHA! PHASE will make you want to shout "Profit First works!" from the rooftops. You've got some cash in your PROFIT account, you've paid your quarterly taxes from the TAX account, and life feels a little more under control. You talk about Profit First to anyone who will listen. Using the system is probably not all sunshine and rainbows, but you're now feeling confident enough to get through the challenges as they come up.

It usually takes at least a month to get to this stage, but it can take up to six months or more. After you've seen the cadence of the Profit First method, you'll start to see the magic in it. You'll run payroll without wondering if you have enough funds. You'll make your credit card payment in full without panicking. You'll write a rent check knowing that your OPEX account is fully funded. Small moments like these add up and build your confidence in the system.

If you're at this stage, you feel confident adjusting your allocations each quarter and are on the way to reaching your TAPs. Our clients often say something like, "I've never had this much money in my bank accounts, this is awesome!" or "I've never had enough money to pay my taxes in full and on time before!"

When you stick with Profit First through the early stages, you'll reap rewards you never before thought possible. Kate Fish needed accountability to feel comfortable with the process. She wanted someone to walk her through the ups and downs of implementation so she wouldn't be tempted to quit when it got tough. She decided to work with my team to make sure she was doing things right and had ongoing support. Kate had wanted to bypass CAPs and start with TAPs. Luckily, she decided to trust the process and made small changes over the next year, which has allowed her to grow her practice in a sustainable way.

These days, Kate can get a little emotional when she thinks about the fact that she has such a big business. In the vulnerable moments when she wonders, *What if the ball drops? What if everybody just stops coming to work tomorrow? Or what if clients stop coming to the practice?* She reminds herself that she doesn't have to live in fear. Knowing the business has tens of thousands of dollars in savings gives her so much more confidence.

Kate started her practice with a $4,000 loan from her parents and never imagined being in the healthy financial position she is today.

ACCEPTANCE AND DELIGHT: MY LIFE WILL NEVER BE THE SAME

PROFIT FIRST IS YOUR LIFESTYLE now. You know it works, and you see the results with your own eyes when you look at your bank accounts: It's time to reward yourself at your next profit distribution.

Profit First will evolve over time with you and your business. And over time, you'll be more in tune with the ebbs and flows of money in your business. You'll look at your allocations and reevaluate your goals and priorities quarterly, but otherwise, you'll be able to go into cruise control mode between quarterly reviews. If an emergency comes up or a huge expansion opportunity presents itself, you'll know to revisit your allocations off-cycle.

For Alison Pidgeon, MA, LPC, owner of Move Forward Counseling in Pennsylvania, it took a good three to four months to get things smoothed out. The first few months weren't exactly hard, but there were some challenges to contend with, like bigger annual expenses (hello, liability insurance) that hadn't been planned for and couldn't be covered in full by the OpEx account.

After about six months implementing the Profit First method in her practice, another client, Cathy Ranieri, MA, LCPC, owner of Lakeshore Counseling Group in Illinois, shared this: "I think that one of the big takeaways for me is that there's always enough. There's always enough money to cover all your expenses, to cover your tax liability. And knowing that just gives me a lot of peace."

Each phase of Profit First adoption will take some time to move through. You might spend a few months hovering between Excitement, Resistance, and Overwhelm. This is normal, a part of the process. If you find yourself stuck in the Resistance or Overwhelm stage, email me at info@profitfirstfortherapists. com. You can also find lots of support and accountability resources at www.profitfirstfortherapists.com/tools.

After college, I decided that I would ride a motorcycle instead of buying a car. I signed up for a motorcycle course at the local community college and started the following Saturday. I was the only woman in the class, but that just made me want it more. Even though I haven't ridden a motorcycle in twenty years, I vividly remember one of the instructor's tips from day one: "If you're starting to get wobbly and feel like you're going to fall, just accelerate a little and the motorcycle will straighten out." If you hit the brakes, you will fall. I've tried both strategies many times, and both are true. Since then, I've found that my motorcycle instructor's lesson applies to many things in life. It definitely applies to Profit First. If you're feeling wobbly, don't hit the brakes and stop; commit to the process and double down until things even out. Even if you have to temporarily change one of your allocations to 0%, keep going. Even if you need a quick infusion of cash, keep going. (We'll talk more about debt in Chapter 12.)

What will the next twelve months look like in your Profit First journey? It really depends on where you started. If you already had healthy reserves in your business bank accounts, you may not notice a big difference. If you were struggling with cash flow, it might take several months to rectify the situation and get your debt paid down. That's all okay.

TAKE ACTION: GET REAL WITH YOUR SUPPORT TEAM—AND YOURSELF

IF YOU WORK WITH AN accountant or bookkeeper, it's time to let them know that you will be implementing Profit First in your business. The response you get might vary, from a high five to a grumble and a furrowed brow or anything in between. Schedule a meeting and let your accountant know that you want to go over your expenses in detail so they will be prepared to go over the nitty-gritty with you. Discuss your estimated tax liability and how much you expect to owe at the end of the year. This data will prepare you to update your Instant Assessment and start taking your profit first. If your accountant's response isn't positive, stand firm. You can do this with or without them, and after they see the results, they will be a believer.

I mentioned earlier that Profit First is a journey, not a destination. It can be easy to veer off course when you're embarking on any kind of long-term project, especially if your accountant or bookkeeper isn't excited about the change. If you could benefit from having someone keep you in check, visit www.profitfirstfortherapists.com/tools to check out the accountability resources. You'll also find some tips there on how to find the right accountant or bookkeeper for you.

CHAPTER 7

What to Do When Things Go Wrong: Common Mistakes and Solutions

IN THE LAST CHAPTER, I shared the Five Emotional Phases of Profit First: Excitement, Resistance, Overwhelm, Aha!, and Acceptance and Delight. As you build your Profit First system, there's a good chance something will go wrong, and you might even be tempted to quit. This specifically tends to happen in the Overwhelm stage. Don't give up, because the Aha! phase is right around the corner. It's a fact of life: Everyone makes mistakes.

In this chapter, I'll review the most common ways your Profit First journey can get off track and make suggestions for tackling each issue.

MISTAKE #1: SKIPPING THE BANK ACCOUNTS

IT CAN BE REALLY TEMPTING to skip opening up the bank accounts and just do Profit First "on paper." Some variations I've seen include keeping one checking account and using an Excel spreadsheet to allocate funds to each category, adding subaccounts in QuickBooks to pretend there are multiple bank accounts, and even doing the allocations on paper. News flash: Because you're a human, you'll still check your bank account regularly and see one large sum of money that you'll want to spend. It's how we are all wired.

I rarely see the pretend bank accounts work in real life. It's incredibly easy to borrow from an account when you don't even need to go through the effort of a bank transfer.

Quincee Gideon, PsyD, owner of Woven Together Trauma Therapy in California, didn't skip all the bank accounts; she decided to combine the OpEx and Payroll accounts so she would have fewer accounts to deal with. Profit First worked for her practice, but she felt as though she didn't have quite enough money and couldn't put her finger on why. After it became clear that the combined account wasn't working, Kelly from my team suggested she open a new Payroll bank account. When Quincee agreed, we knew it would be helpful for her to see where the money was going, but it turned out to be a complete game changer. That small alteration made a world of difference for Quincee. She gained clarity around what was happening in her business and a better understanding of the inner workings of her practice. Since Quincee opened the Payroll account, there is enough money in each bank account, she's paid off her credit card, and she's been able to increase her own salary.

MISTAKE #2: NOT FUNDING THE ACCOUNTS ENOUGH UP FRONT

When you first implement Profit First, you'll take the amount in your checking account and divide it among your new bank accounts. You might be tempted to slide as much as you can into the PROFIT or TAX account. As nice as that might seem, I want you to have enough funds in each account to make it to your next transfer date, so funding accounts correctly is important. Remember, you won't be adding funds until your next transfer date, which might be one to two weeks away, even as far off as a month away.

When you don't have enough money in your accounts, it's like starting a race with both hands tied behind your back. You might make it, but it'll be much harder than it needs to be. As you're planning your initial transfers, consider all of your upcoming expenses. What will you need to pay from each account between now and the next transfer date? How much do you need for payroll? To pay your credit cards? To cover rent? Each account should have enough to cover the expenses that keep your business running.

MISTAKE #3: BORROWING FROM ACCOUNTS

THIS MISTAKE OFTEN FOLLOWS MISTAKE #2. If your Profit First accounts weren't properly funded, you'll need to transfer funds so your account balances don't fall below zero. Obviously, bouncing payments is not good and we certainly want to avoid that. Lack of money is a symptom, and you must find the cause or you'll end up in the same place a few weeks from now.

For an insurance-based practice, this can come up if or when insurance payments temporarily stop coming in. This is common, and the major reason I sometimes recommend adding an EMERGENCY account. (More on that in Chapter 8.) If you have an insurance-based practice, cash flow ups and downs are sometimes out of your control. I'd rather you borrow from the account that's meant for emergencies than raid your TAX account. Taking your own tax money is essentially stealing from yourself. Don't do it!

MISTAKE #4: TRANSFERRING OFF SCHEDULE

IT'S COMPLETELY FINE TO TRANSFER a few days early if you are going on vacation or will be out of the office. But if you need to move funds between your scheduled transfers, look at the information your bank accounts are giving you. Have you been overspending? Has your business grown, and your allocations no longer work as a result? If you're in a period where cash is tight, consider moving to a weekly transfer schedule instead of moving money haphazardly. If that doesn't work, it's time to go back to the Instant Assessment and see if your allocations should change.

When the balance of one of your accounts gets low, your business is trying to tell you something: An area of your business is no longer aligned with your allocations. You'll need to change your spending habits or your allocations.

MISTAKE #5: STARTING WITH ALLOCATIONS THAT ARE TOO HIGH

IN ALL THE PROFIT FIRST implementations I have worked on, I can't think of one where the practice owner said, "Let's start my *Profit* allocation at one percent." It makes sense: You should be paid well for the work you do, so almost everyone wants to start their allocation as high as possible.

When you start with allocations that are significantly different from where your business is today, massive changes need to be made immediately. That's just hard, and it's why I like to start with small incremental changes that give your business time to adapt to its new normal. I'd rather start with 1% in your PROFIT and TAX accounts than put your business at risk.

I encourage you to start slow and make steady progress. This approach significantly increases the likelihood that you will stick to the plan. It's okay to start slow. You might be at 1% *Profit* today, but you won't stay there forever.

MISTAKE #6: NOT CHANGING YOUR SPENDING

PROFIT FIRST WILL BRING AREAS where you might be over-spending to light. For the system to work, you must be willing to reduce expenses or increase your revenue without increasing your spending. I know, this probably sounds so obvious—but years of Profit First implementation confirm that it's not. It's easy to justify most expenses to yourself, but your bank account won't lie to you.

Sometimes this mistake happens in your personal life as well. If you tend to treat your business like a piggy bank and take out cash whenever you need it, that will likely cause cash flow issues in the business at some point. The same applies if you're taking more money out of the business than it can reasonably sustain. If that's the case, it's a good time to look at your personal spending to see if there are any areas where you might be able to cut back.

If you think this might be your issue, in Chapter 9, I'll show you how to reverse-engineer your practice to generate your desired take-home pay.

MISTAKE #7: RELYING ON THE PROFIT DISTRIBUTION TO COVER YOUR PERSONAL EXPENSES

THE FUNDS THAT ACCUMULATE IN your PROFIT account are your reward for being a shareholder of your practice. Each quarter, you'll distribute half the funds in the account to yourself, just as a public company pays quarterly dividends. If you rely on this account to put food on the table for your family, you may find yourself living dangerously close to the edge.

Cherie had a small group practice and allocated a significant amount to her OWNER'S PAY account. But it just wasn't enough to cover her day-to-day living expenses. She charged so much to her personal credit cards during each quarter that they were almost maxed out by the time her quarterly profit distribution came around, and her entire profit went to paying them off.

Cherie wasn't proud of this, so my team only found out when we started discussing expansion plans. At that point, we suggested a temporary reduction of the *Profit* allocation. "Wait," Cherie said, "I can't do that. I need the profit, or I won't be able to pay off my credit cards." Her business was covering her personal expenses, barely, but there wasn't a penny to spare to invest in growth or expansion. If she wanted to grow the practice, she'd have to reduce her personal spending or get very creative.

Your OWNER'S PAY account and your paycheck (if applicable) should ideally cover your personal day-to-day expenses. If not and your *Profit* allocation is still at 1%, it's time to look at what you can cut from your personal expenses or what you can cut in the business.

If you find yourself wanting to take money from the PROFIT account between quarterly distributions, you may want to review your allocations. It's possible that the *Owner's Pay* allocation needs to be higher to cover your personal expenses and *Profit* needs to be lower. Both accounts serve you, the business owner, so it's okay to reallocate to support yourself. Your quarterly profit distribution is intended for celebrations, or bonus items like a trip or something extravagant you wouldn't usually buy for yourself. As your business grows, your overall lifestyle will improve as well and with time, your *Owner's Pay* and *Profit* allocations will increase.

MISTAKE #8: FORGETTING THAT PROFIT IS A HABIT, NOT AN EVENT

THERE MAY BE DAYS WHEN Profit First doesn't feel easy or seems like it's just not working. Some weeks will feel great, some weeks you might feel like giving up, and other times you might fall off the wagon. The key is to not give up. Get back up, get back in the game and the work will pay off.

Taking your profit first is a habit, not an event. Just as I can't go for one run and be ready for a marathon, you may not be able to make your transfers once and set your profit on cruise control.

For me, money habits come easily; it's the workout habits I must always work on. For the last few years, I have been running with a local group on Mondays and Wednesdays because they keep me accountable and it takes one more decision off my plate. I don't have to plan which days I'll run; it's always Monday and Wednesday. These runs are on my calendar, and they have become a habit. I go whether it's too hot or too cold, whether I feel like it or not. I'm a slow, slow runner. But I show up for one hour twice each week and put one foot in front of the other, no matter what.

Now, a Profit First habit won't take you an hour twice each week. It should take about fifteen minutes or less each time you transfer. Put the transfers on your calendar and find an accountability buddy or group if you need support to stay on track. When it feels hard, your group will remind you of why you're doing this in the first place. They will also celebrate your wins and your Profit First distributions with you. Need help with accountability? Visit www.profitfirstfortherapists.com/tools.

MISTAKE # 9: NOT ADJUSTING ALLOCATIONS ON A REGULAR BASIS

I LOVE CHECKING THINGS OFF my to-do list and feeling "done." If you feel like you just want to sprint to the finish line, I completely relate. When it comes to Profit First, I've had to change my mindset to accept that the system is a journey, not a destination, and it's never quite done. We can't just "set it and forget it" like the '90s infomercials promised. Even after years of implementation, I review my own allocations quarterly and update them as needed, and my team and I do the same for our clients. As a business grows, it's sometimes necessary to take one step back to take two steps forward.

Alison Pidgeon, whom you met in Chapter 6, learned this lesson when her business grew rapidly. The allocations that had moved her through the intense growth period weren't working at all anymore. A big jump in income (and profit) meant the *Tax* allocation wasn't cutting it and needed to be increased because a larger portion of her income was in a higher tax bracket.

For another client, Kristen Breese, LCPC, owner of Counseling Works in Illinois, we had to completely change allocations after she added another location to her practice. She had shifted from hiring less experienced clinicians with lower commissions to hiring more experienced clinicians at higher commissions. She was still well within our recommended ratios, but the allocations that had worked six months before just didn't make sense anymore.

I share this with you so you know that if your allocations don't work, it's okay to change them. The system still works, but your business needs have changed and the allocations need to change as well.

MISTAKE #10: IGNORING YOUR ACCOUNTING

MANY PRACTICE OWNERS THINK OF accounting as an inconvenience they face at the end of the year for the sole purpose of filing their taxes. They'll slog through their bank statements, electronic health record (EHR) reports, and a pile of 1099s all at once to piece things together and work on their taxes.

When you do your accounting regularly, whether on a spreadsheet or accounting software, you'll have access to financial information that gives you incredible insight into your practice. Your numbers have a story to tell, if you'll listen. They'll tell you which months are your busiest and which are your slowest. They'll remind you that your liability insurance payment is due in March each year. They'll show you that your overhead has been creeping up.

Through Profit First, you'll review your bank balances at least once each month, which will be incredibly helpful. You'll have a pulse on the movement of money in your practice. I encourage you to review your financials at least once each month so you don't get too far behind. When you do, look at your P&L and balance sheet so you can pair that data with what you see in your bank accounts.

MISTAKE #11: GIVING IN TO TEMPTATION TO SPEND

As you implement Profit First, you'll notice quickly that two of your accounts have ever-increasing balances: Profit and Tax. For some practice owners, it can be tempting to dip into these accounts "just this once"—which turns into pilfering profit before the quarterly distribution. These funds are for your benefit, so don't steal from yourself. Do everything in your power not to spend that money until it's time for either your quarterly profit distribution, or estimated tax payments.

Over the years, I've seen lots of business owners take money out of their TAX accounts for things that aren't tax-related. And more often than not, that puts them in a difficult situation at tax time. Last year, a client was ecstatic when we ran a year-end tax estimate in the fourth quarter. For the first time, she had more than enough money to pay her tax bill! So she proceeded to take out a large sum, thinking it wasn't needed—forgetting that a first quarter estimated tax payment would also be due on April 15. Suddenly, there wasn't enough money to cover both the previous year's balance and the first quarter estimate. I highly recommend waiting until you have your final tax return in hand and are certain that you have enough money to pay your estimated tax before taking anything out of your TAX account.

In some instances, you may find you have saved more than you need in your TAX account. When that happens, you'll get a bonus profit distribution *after* you've confirmed that all your tax payments are covered.

MISTAKE #12: NOT TAKING YOUR PROFIT DISTRIBUTION

IF YOU'RE A SAVER, YOU may want to leave your profit in the business "just in case." This is your hard-earned money; you deserve it. Each quarter, take half the funds in your PROFIT account and transfer them to your personal bank account or use it to pay down debt.

If you find yourself reinvesting your profit in the business, you don't really have a PROFIT account. If you are using the funds for growth, I would invite you to create an EXPANSION account instead (I cover this account in more detail in Chapter 8) and allocate a percentage of your income to the account each time you transfer funds. I'd like for your PROFIT account to be truly for you, a reward for the hard work you do as a shareholder of the business. Treat yourself to something nice: a fancy meal, a special outing, or something you have been wanting to buy like shoes, a bag, a game, etc.

MISTAKE #13: ADDING COMPLEXITY TO THE SYSTEM

PROFIT FIRST DOESN'T HAVE TO be complicated to work, even though it might feel complex to you right now. After my team and I implement the system, some of our clients almost can't believe how simple it truly is and start looking for ways to overcomplicate things. There's no need to overthink it. Profit First really can be simple after you get the hang of it.

One common way I see therapists complicate the system is by being too rigid with it. If an allocation isn't working, change it. Even if you are intentional about the growth in your practice, there will be times when you simply need to temporarily spend more on something like rent or an additional admin, and you *can* change your allocations to reflect that. If you want (or don't want) a vault account at another bank, that's okay, too. I'd rather you keep iterating than give up on Profit First altogether.

MISTAKE #14: THROWING MONEY AT PROBLEMS

ON THE ONE HAND, I'M a firm believer in the adage, "If you have enough money to solve a problem, you don't have a problem." On the other hand, not all problems deserve your money.

Profit First will expose inefficiencies in your financial processes as well as other areas of your business. If the problem exposed is a process issue that could be solved with automation through software, that is money well spent. For example, if you can reduce friction for a potential new client by adding online scheduling to your website and removing the need for them to call, leave a message, and wait for a call back, that is money well spent that will also reduce your long-term admin costs. If you approached the same problem by hiring a full-time receptionist to sit in your office and wait for the phone to ring, it would be an inefficient use of your money.

There are times when you'll *need* to throw money at a problem, like if your biller quits unexpectedly and you need to bring in a more expensive replacement to temporarily fill the gap until you can find someone new. That's a short-term expense for a critical function in your business.

Throwing money at long-term problems takes a different level of analysis and consideration. Before you do this, look at your Profit First accounts and see what you can afford. Will you need to make cuts in another area to afford this new expense? What is the long-term commitment? The way you approach the problem, and the cost, will differ based on your answers.

MISTAKE #15: NOT MEASURING THE RETURN ON INVESTMENT (ROI)

COACHES, MARKETING, WEBSITES, ETC.: THE opportunities to invest in your business are endless. If you are investing in something with a significant price tag, you should measure the results. A return on investment means that your practice will generate more revenue after adding an expense, not less. ROI isn't always easy to measure because it's not just black or white. It might take several weeks for an investment to produce a result. For example, if you spend $500/month on a new ad campaign, a positive ROI would be getting eight new clients from the campaign. A negative ROI would be getting zero new clients from the campaign. But what if you got sixteen inquiries and only converted two new clients? That's mostly good, but could be better. Is the issue the ad or the conversion? This is a gray area that requires some discernment.

Marketing is necessary, but if you don't have a good way to track incoming referrals and convert them to clients, spending money on marketing isn't always a good investment.

If you track the metrics in your practice, it will be easier to identify what is working and what isn't. Are clients completing their treatment plans? Are they coming to their intake appointments, never to be seen again? What percentage of callers convert to clients? For the callers who don't schedule, why not? Are they looking for a specialty your practice doesn't have? Do they have a brand of insurance that you don't accept? A solo practice owner might know this information instinctively, but the larger a practice becomes, the more challenging it is to know what's going on.

If you are spending big money on advertising and don't know the answers to these questions, your money might be better spent coaching your clinicians on laying the groundwork for long-term client relationships. As an example, many of the group practice owners my team and I work with expect their clinicians to see clients for an average of eight to twelve visits before they end therapy. Ultimately, you are the best judge of what your clients need to be successful. If a clinician is below the average, there is an opportunity to coach around retention in addition to or instead of spending more money on marketing.

You don't have to measure the ROI of every single expense in your business; that would be too time consuming. Start with the largest expenses on your P&L and do a few each month to get in the habit. This exercise will point you to which expenses to cut or keep, and you'll continue to make your practice as efficient as possible.

WHEN YOU *SHOULDN'T* START PROFIT FIRST

I KNOW, I KNOW, THIS book is about Profit First. So why would I tell you *not* to try it? I truly believe that Profit First can help every therapist out there, but I've also seen the harsh reality of implementing this amazing system with clients in a variety of situations. Because of that, I believe that there are times when you may need to make a few changes to your practice *before* you start to set yourself up for success. Profit First isn't a magic wand, so if you are in one of the following three situations, I have a little homework for you before you get started.

1. **Your expenses are much higher than your income.**

   If you find yourself taking out loans regularly to make ends meet, starting Profit First is a little like being in a canoe that is filling up with water and using a bucket to empty the water while there is still a hole in the hull. I'm not exactly an outdoorsy person, but my canoeing experience at summer camp taught me that it's much better to plug the hole, and *then* use the bucket to empty the water. I highly suggest that you plug the hole in your proverbial canoe first. That means cutting expenses, increasing revenue, or, in many cases, both before you start Profit First.

2. **You regularly bounce payments in your business checking account.**

   If cash is so tight that you regularly rack up NSF fees, splitting your money among five or six accounts will only make things worse. You won't have enough money to properly fund the accounts up front (Mistake #2), which will set you up for failure. You need to make some changes, and fast, but setting up Profit First during this difficult time will only restrict your cash further.

3. You are not ready to make changes and allocate some time to improving your financial situation.

Profit First will make you take an honest look at your financial life and spending. If you're not ready to spend time reviewing expenses, canceling subscriptions, and tackling your finances, it's best to hold off for now. Profit First won't take a huge time investment, but it will take about fifteen minutes of your undivided attention each transfer day to calculate transfers and thirty to sixty minutes each quarter to review your allocations.

If your practice is in any of the three preceding scenarios, you can still greatly benefit from reading this book. You can still work through the exercises to see where you might be overspending or which expense categories might be out of line. You can still open your Profit First bank accounts, too, but don't start using them quite yet. For now, your *Profit, Tax,* and *Owner's Pay* allocations might temporarily be zero. You can do this, and the tools in this book will give you helpful information about your practice and a path for success.

CHAPTER 8

Advanced Profit First for Complex Situations

IF YOU'RE FEELING LIKE PROFIT First might not work for your business because your situation is more complex than others I have described so far, you likely need to use at least one of the Advanced Profit First techniques instead. These techniques cover almost every challenge my team and I have experienced when implementing Profit First with our clients.

ADDITIONAL BANK ACCOUNTS

SOMETIMES THE PROFIT FIRST FOUNDATIONAL bank accounts aren't enough, and adding one or more additional bank accounts can further customize the system to your needs. If there is a specific expense that stresses you out or feels daunting, give it its own bank account and allocation. Some examples of helpful additional accounts are:

- **EXPANSION:** The EXPANSION account should be used when planning to move to a larger location, when adding a location, when there is a need to replace a significant amount of furniture, or when planning leasehold improvements to the existing space (e.g., repainting the whole office, changing the carpet, etc.). I'll go over scaling a practice in much more detail in Chapter 13, but this account can help a practice save up and prepare for expansion.

- **EMERGENCY:** In my experience, a sense of financial security is important to many private practice owners. I find that having a rainy-day fund within the business can really help alleviate the financial stress. If that rings true to you, add the EMERGENCY account to your list. This account doesn't need a specific goal; it's like an insurance policy or your own self-funded line of credit for the business. As the balance grows, you can decide to use some of this money for expansion or a new team member if you wish. When a new idea comes to you, you'll have the freedom (and cash) to explore it. This account especially makes sense for insurance-based practices, those with salaried team members, or for practice owners who feel more comfortable with an extra cushion of protection. This is a "peace of mind" account.

- **FUTURE EMPLOYEE:** This account makes sense for practices that are new to hiring or planning to hire for a brand-new role, like practice manager or clinical director. In situations where there's a significant up-front cost to hiring (e.g., no insurance income for at least a few weeks) it's a good idea to have two to six weeks' worth of the employee's wages and payroll tax saved up. This reduces the stress around trying to fill the caseload right away and helps ensure that you and your new employee will be provided for financially. If you open this account a few months prior to your very first hire, it can later become your PAYROLL account.

- **BONUS:** If you have a bonus structure in place for your team, it makes sense to set the funds aside throughout the year so you don't raid your PROFIT account at bonus time. If your team members earn their bonus, you'll have the cash for it. Pay the employees who *did* earn it and keep the remainder as a bonus for you. You can move the remaining funds to PROFIT!

- **PAID TIME OFF (PTO)/SICK TIME:** We are seeing an increasing number of practices offer PTO as a benefit, in part because some states and cities require a minimum amount of sick time each year. There is a double "hit" when you offer PTO because there is no revenue generated for the business when a clinician isn't working but you still have to cover payroll. If team members accrue PTO each pay period, you can use a PTO account to save up for the days when your team uses their benefit.

- **ANNUAL EXPENSES:** For some practices, large annual expenses can put a strain on the OPEX account. When we use an ANNUAL EXPENSES account, we estimate how much money will be needed for larger recurring items like liability insurance, professional association dues, and licensing fees, and then calculate a CAP for the account. When the annual payment for each item is due, you'll transfer the appropriate amount from the ANNUAL EXPENSES account to the OPEX account and pay the bill from OPEX. For example, if this account must cover insurance ($1,500), annual software fees ($1,200), and association dues ($850), the goal will be to allocate $3,550/year or $296/month to the ANNUAL EXPENSES account. When the insurance payment is due, $1,500 will be transferred from ANNUAL EXPENSES to OPEX.

- **CEU/EDUCATION REIMBURSEMENT:** Many practice owners allocate a specific dollar amount toward continuing education reimbursement for each team member (I typically see amounts anywhere from $250–$1,000/ year). With a team, this can add up, so a separate account is an easy way to make sure you're always covered.

- **DEBT:** When there is a significant amount of debt in the business, I often recommend using a DEBT bank account or allocation. The percentage allocated can either be used to immediately pay down debt at the time of each transfer, or it can grow in the DEBT account to cover monthly debt payments and additional principal payments.

- **ADDITIONAL ACCOUNTS AS NEEDED:** You get the point; you can add a bank account for anything that is helpful to your business. For example, Jessica Tappana, MSW, LCSW, owner of Aspire Counseling in Missouri, has a RENT account. Her landlord takes a long time to cash each rent check, and it was stressing Jessica out because she couldn't always remember if her OpEx balance was truly high or if her landlord had just forgotten to cash a check or two. With a RENT account, the funds are out of sight and out of mind and there's always enough to cover the rent check when it is (finally) cashed.

ADDING INCOME STREAMS

MANY PRACTICE OWNERS WISH TO add income streams to their lives, in part because this can allow them to make passive income. If this is something you are considering, there are a few things you'll need to keep in mind related to structuring your accounting and implementing Profit First.

Often, the "testing" phase of a new income stream is done as an extension of an existing private practice through a DBA (doing business as) for a few weeks or months until it's ready to stand on its own. This can be done by registering a fictitious name or DBA with the secretary of state in the state where your business is registered. It's always a good idea to talk to an attorney before you add a new business to your private practice. Some questions you should discuss with them include:

- Is a DBA sufficient, or should you create a separate legal entity?
- Does the work you do in your second business create a liability for your license or your practice?
- Will the work you do in your second business be subject to review by your state licensing board?
- Are there state or local restrictions that you should be aware of?

I'm not an attorney, but you can see how important it is to consider the previous questions before mixing two businesses together.

If you decide to separate the businesses legally, you'll want to separate everything else as well: state registration, IRS Employer Identification Number (EIN), bank accounts, accounting records, etc.

From a tax perspective, if you start a second business under the umbrella of your established business using a DBA, the profit from both businesses will be reported on one tax return.

If you'd like to add an income stream but don't have an established second business yet, give yourself a budget and a separate OpEx bank account where you'll transfer the allocated startup funds. For example, if you are creating online training courses for sale, the expenses for your new venture should be paid from a new TRAINING – OpEx account. Let's say you want to launch an online training program for millennials dealing with career changes. You'll need a course-hosting platform to manage the content, registrations, etc. When you sign up for the platform, the expense should be paid by your TRAINING – OPEX account. If you're using your practice email or existing software subscriptions to get started, these expenses can stay entirely in the practice. No need to split hairs; just the new expenses get paid from this account.

If you use a separate account during the "testing" phase and regularly transfer funds from your private practice or personal account, you'll have a much better sense of how much money you have invested, and whether or not the venture is profitable.

When your investment amount is a deliberate decision, you won't feel guilty about spending money on software, design, or marketing to get the project off the ground, and you'll see clearly how much money is left.

Once your training program is ready for sale, it's time to open a TRAINING – INCOME account. When revenue comes in for course sales, deposit the funds to this new account.

Kanesha had been steadily adding funds to her EXPANSION account for just that: growth. When she first opened the account, she didn't have a specific plan; she just knew that she would want to grow the practice at some point. When she decided to open a therapeutic yoga studio in addition to her group practice, she looked at the account as a sort of bank for the new business that would complement her private practice. Kanesha took a small portion of the funds in her EXPANSION account to launch the new business and bypassed a bank loan altogether. She used the funds to pay her yoga instructors for meetings and training and to get the infrastructure set up for the online studio. What a great feeling!

MOVING FROM SOLO TO GROUP PRACTICE

IN A TRANSITION FROM SOLO to small group practice, most Profit First allocations will change. The biggest difference will be the addition of a TAP for *Payroll – Therapists*. You'll use this allocation whether you decide to hire employees or contractors. The key here is to start moving toward your new TAPs before your first hire, as this will give you a buffer with which to pay your new clinician.

You'll need a PAYROLL account if you don't already have one, so it's time to go back to the bank (before your new hire's first day). If you have already been saving in an EXPANSION or FUTURE EMPLOYEE account, you can move those funds to your new PAYROLL account.

With each new hire, revisit the Instant Assessment to see if any changes are needed. Here's an example of how CAPs will change during the transition from a solo practice to a small group practice with one full-time clinician. In the example in Table 8.1, I estimate that the new clinician will generate approximately $8,000 per month in revenue (16 sessions/week x 4 weeks x $125/session) and that their compensation will be around 55% of that amount. I also included an increase in *OpEx* for additional rent, marketing, and software. The *Owner's Pay* allocation holds steady at $8,000/month, but you'll notice that it now represents 40% of income instead of the 67% the same amount represented in the solo practice.

	Solo		Owner + 1 PT Clinician	
	Actual	**CAPs**	**Actual**	**CAPs**
Real Revenue	12,000		20,000	
OpEx – Operating Expenses	1,450	12%	3,100	16%
Payroll – Therapists	0	0%	4,400	22%
Payroll – Admin	0	0%	0	0%
Payroll – Leadership (if applicable)	0	0%	0	0%
Payroll – Owner (if applicable)	0	0%	0	0%
Owner's Pay (if applicable)	8,000	66%	8,000	40%
Tax	500	4%	1,000	5%
Profit	2,050	17%	3,500	17%
Totals	0	100%	0	100%

Table 8.1: Solo vs. Small Group Practice Comparison

If you're wondering about *how much* to pay each therapist, and how to structure their compensation, Chapter 10 has answers for you.

TRANSITIONING FROM A SMALL GROUP TO A LARGER GROUP PRACTICE

THE TRANSITION TO A LARGER group practice brings change as well. As the owner, you will have to pivot from doing a significant amount of the practice's clinical work to managing a team of clinicians. Allocations often change when this happens. Some practice owners can't wait to drop clinical hours and sometimes do so too soon, whereas others hold onto their caseload for dear life and risk burnout. As owners reduce their clinical hours, payroll costs for therapists continue to increase because they are doing most of the clinical work and generating most of the income.

If you revisit the medium and large group practice TAPs from Chapter 2, you'll notice that the *Owner's Pay* allocation goes down sharply between a small group and a medium group. That's because the percentage of the work done by the owner decreases. For example, in a small group practice of one owner and one part-time clinician, the owner might see twenty-five clients each week, while the part-time team member sees sixteen clients each week. That is a total of forty-one sessions per week, of which 61% are done by the owner. Based on those numbers, it makes sense for the owner to take a significant amount of the practice revenue as *Owner's Pay*.

As you continue to add more clinicians, you'll run this calculation again and continue to make adjustments. Once you reach the medium practice size, starting at around $400,000–$500,000 in annual revenue, you'll notice that the allocations stabilize and you won't have to make changes nearly as often.

If we look at a medium group example, the owner might see only fifteen clients each week because they have reduced their caseload, whereas the five full-time clinicians each see twenty-five clients per week. The total weekly session count is 140, of which the owner sees 10.7%. It makes sense for the owner to get a smaller percentage of overall income as *Owner's Pay* in this case because the practice revenue is much larger and the owner's contribution is smaller. The *Owner's Pay* percentage is smaller because the practice revenue is much larger; it's a smaller piece of a bigger pie. You probably won't make less money in dollars during this transition, but the TAP for *Owner's Pay* will go down.

Let's compare a small group practice with a medium group practice. Our previous medium group example has 140 sessions each week, which generates $70,000 in revenue each month (140 sessions/week x 4 weeks/month x $125/session = $70,000). The owner still sees clients, but most sessions are done by clinician employees, so we need to allocate 50% of income to *Payroll – Therapists*. This practice has added an administrative assistant to help with intake and billing. The owner received a raise in *Owner's Pay*, but that amount only represents 12.9% of the practice revenue.

	Owner + 1 PT Clinician		Group of 5 FT Clinicians + Owner	
	Actual	CAPs	Actual	CAPs
Real Revenue	20,500		70,000	
OpEx – Operating Expenses	3,100	15%	11,300	16%
Payroll – Therapists	4,400	22%	35,000	50%
Payroll – Admin	0	0%	4,200	6%
Payroll – Leadership (if applicable)	0	0%	0	0%
Payroll – Owner (if applicable)	0	0%	0	0%
Owner's Pay (if applicable)	8,000	39%	9,000	13%
Tax	1,500	7%	4,700	7%
Profit	3,500	17%	5,800	8%
Totals	0	100%	0	100%

Table 8.2: Small Group Practice vs. Medium Group Practice Comparison

As the practice grows, if the allocations suddenly feel like they aren't working anymore, change them. Go back to the Instant Assessment and update your revenue and expenses, and then compare that to the medium group practice target allocations (from the TAPs chart in Appendix 4).

PROFIT FIRST FOR MULTIPLE BUSINESSES

PRACTICE OWNERS OFTEN ASK ME, "How does Profit First work if I own more than one business?" Maybe you have a private practice *and* a coaching business, membership group, or online course. Your second business could even be something completely unrelated to private practice. You'll want to consider both the accounting and legal implications when deciding how to proceed.

Following Profit First to the letter, if you own three businesses, you could end up with fifteen (or more) bank accounts.

One trick you can use to simplify the Profit First system in this situation is to open only one TAX and one PROFIT account as personal bank accounts (in your personal name) instead of having a TAX and PROFIT account for each business. When it's time to transfer funds, each business contributes to your personal accounts.

For example: If Business A has an allocation of $1,850 to the TAX account this week, it transfers $1,850 from Business A's INCOME account to the personal TAX account.

If Business B has an allocation of $380 to the TAX account this week, it transfers $380 from Business B's INCOME account to the personal Tax account. The balance of the TAX account is $2,230 after both transfers have occurred.

You still get the benefit of Profit First by having INCOME, OPEX, OWNER'S PAY, and/or PAYROLL accounts for each business, but you have the advantage of paying taxes from one account.

If you have a TAX account for each business, you're likely to transfer funds back and forth between the accounts to combine them before you make a tax payment, and it's easy to make a mistake. If the funds aren't in the right account when your payment processes, you'll owe the IRS a penalty. Having one TAX account instead of multiple ones means you won't have to move money back and forth between accounts or wake up in a cold sweat in the middle of the night, wondering if you scheduled your tax payment correctly.

One of our clients with two businesses once scheduled his quarterly estimated tax payment from Business A in advance, but thought it was scheduled from Business B. When September 15 came around, his third-quarter payment bounced because the funds were in the wrong bank account. He was understandably frustrated because he did everything right and had the funds saved but still missed his quarterly payment.

We can use personal bank accounts for the TAX and PROFIT accounts only because they are accounts that benefit you, the owner. You should *not* use personal bank accounts for any of the other Profit First accounts.

With most business entities in the US, you personally owe tax at the end of the year; through Profit First, your business pays the tax on your behalf. If you are a sole proprietor or own an LLC, partnership, or an S corporation (or any entity taxed as an S corporation), the business itself does not pay tax at the federal level. Rather, the profit flows through to your personal tax return, where it is taxed. You're achieving the same goal with one TAX account: the businesses pay taxes on your behalf by contributing funds to your personal TAX account instead of keeping the funds in the business.

When you combine your profit from multiple businesses into one PROFIT account, you still get a quarterly profit distribution of 50% of the balance. The remaining balance serves as a secondary emergency fund, for true emergencies.

A note of caution: Combining the profit of both businesses doesn't mean that you should dip into the PROFIT account to cover one business with funds from the other! If you'll be tempted to do this, a combined account is not the right solution for you, and you should open the five foundational accounts for each business. Also, as your taxable income grows with the combined revenue of both businesses, you might move up to a higher tax bracket. In that case, you'll want to update your tax allocation.

Combined accounts can make it more challenging to notice that something is wrong, so make sure to keep a close eye on your allocations for each business.

MORE THAN ONE BUSINESS OWNER

HAVING MORE THAN ONE OWNER will certainly complicate things a little, and that's okay. There are two common situations where this may occur. The first is a partnership in which two or more individuals own a certain percentage of the business; for example, three owners with 50%/35%/15% ownership. The second common situation is an S corporation in which two or more shareholders each own an even percentage of the business, such as 50%/50% ownership.

Going into business with someone is a long-term decision that is similar to a marriage in many ways. Because it can be so challenging, I encourage you to *truly* discuss your expectations with your partner(s) and consult with a lawyer before starting the business. I'm not talking about discussing marketing strategies and paint colors, but rather the tough conversations like how much you'd like to be paid, how much money you can contribute to start the business, and how much time you are willing to invest in the practice each week. It's easier to have these hard conversations *before* you join your life with someone else's through business ownership. A lot of what you can and cannot do will stem directly from the partnership agreement, so make sure that various scenarios have been discussed and are covered in the agreement.

For example, let's say Partner A sees thirty clients per week and Partner B sees only eight because they handle most of the administrative work for the practice. Is the same percentage of profit still allocated to each partner? You can imagine how quickly resentment might creep in if this kind of scenario hasn't been discussed in advance.

With both partnerships and multi-owner S corporations, legal documents should clearly state how each owner will be paid. That may be a combination of salaries (S corporation), guaranteed payments (partnership), and distributions. When in doubt, your accountant will refer to the legal document for clarity. We often encounter owners who want to pay themselves in a way that's not aligned with the legal document. If things have changed, it's time to update your agreement with an amendment (through your attorney) to ensure that everyone is on the same page.

In a partnership, the OWNER's PAY account needs to serve two or more people, so you will likely need to allocate a larger CAP and TAP to it. This works, because multiple owners of the business do a larger share of the work than a single owner. Two people can see more clients than one can. Consider spending habits as well as personal preferences when you decide whether to have a separate OWNER's PAY account for each partner or shareholder or keep the funds in one account.

When it comes time for your quarterly profit distribution, the profit is distributed based on the percentage of ownership. In the case of our three-person partnership example (with 50%/35%/15% partners), a $10,000 quarterly distribution would mean $5,000 for Partner A, $3,500 for Partner B, and $1,500 for Partner C.

How about your TAX account? It gets even more complicated there. Partnerships and S corporations are flow-through tax entities. Such entities do not pay federal tax; rather, the profit flows to the partner or shareholder's personal tax returns through a K 1. The profit is then taxed on the personal tax return.

Partners and shareholders may have very different personal situations:

- Married/not married
- Kids/no kids
- Additional income/no additional income in the household
- Itemized deductions/standard deduction

Having different tax situations means that partners and shareholders will not necessarily be taxed at the same rate. When that's the case, ideally, you want to cover the largest tax liability among the partners in your *Tax* allocation. When it's time for quarterly estimated tax payments on April 15, June 15, September 15, and January 15, the business distributes the amount in the TAX account based on the percentage of ownership. Yes, that means that some partners may have money left over after they make their tax payments. Huh?

Let's take our S corporation as an example. There are two 50%/50% shareholders. Shareholder A is married and their spouse is a high-income earner. They file their taxes as "married filing jointly" and, based on their combined income, their next dollar earned will be taxed at the 32% federal tax bracket. (I'm only using federal tax for this example, but if your state has an income tax, you would add that as well. Appendix 1 explains progressive tax brackets in more detail.) Shareholder B is single and in the 22% federal tax bracket, based on their income from the practice. Not all of their income will be taxed at 32% or 22%, but the owners can set a goal to allocate $32 to *Tax* and divide $68 between *Owner's Pay* and *Profit* for every $100 available for the owners.

You can see that if you keep things equal, it doesn't have to be overly complicated.

Partners tend to get caught up on this piece because they want the business to pay their taxes and they want their take-home pay to be the same. Why should Shareholder A have less left over than Shareholder B? That's not how tax works, though. Think about a time when you worked for someone as an employee. If you made a salary of $70,000/year and your coworker earned the same salary, was there any guarantee that your take-home pay, after taxes and deductions, would be the same? NO! The same applies for partners and shareholders. Our goal is to keep the distributions in line with the ownership percentages.

CONVERTING FROM AN LLC TO AN S CORPORATION

THE LLC IS A VERSATILE entity, in part because it can be taxed in a few different ways. There may come a point in the LLC's journey when profit is high enough that an S corporation election may reduce taxes. If you have already implemented Profit First in your practice, this can be a confusing transition.

The owner gets paid differently in each scenario: the LLC owner receives an owner's draw (a payment to the owner with no payroll tax withheld), and a S corporation owner receives reasonable compensation* (paid through payroll, with taxes withheld) and an owner's profit distribution. An S corporation owner is both an employee and a shareholder of the business. The reasonable compensation is most commonly a salary that has federal and state tax withheld from the employee (that's you). In addition, the employer pays 50% of Social Security and Medicare on behalf of the employee. The remaining 50% of Social Security and Medicare are withheld from the employee's wages and reflected on the W-2. As a result, the owner no longer needs to pay self-employment tax.

Even if you are the only employee, I highly recommend that you use a reputable payroll service: Penalties are high for missed payments and filings.

During the transition, you'll need to revisit the Instant Assessment and enter a new amount in *Payroll – Owner*. Start with your salary, and then add 10% to that amount to account for payroll taxes. For example, if your salary is $72,000/year, $72,000 + 10% = $79,200. If you used a full year P&L to complete the Instant Assessment, $79,200 should go in the *Payroll – Owner* box, while *Owner's Pay* should be reduced by that amount (or might become 0). Because you will now pay a portion of your taxes through payroll, you may need to revisit your allocations and decrease the *Tax* allocation in order to increase *Payroll – Owner*. That's normal, and it's okay. You or your accountant should recalculate your estimated tax payments to account for this change.

If you already have payroll for your team, keep the service connected to your PAYROLL account. In the Instant Assessment, adjust your *Payroll – Owner* allocation line item to cover your payroll needs as previously calculated. Next, instead of transferring the allocation to a separate bank account, like you did when you used *Owner's Pay*, add it to *Payroll – Therapists, Payroll – Admin,* and *Payroll – Leadership* (from the Instant Assessment) to calculate the total amount to transfer to the PAYROLL account. That's it.

If you are the first and only employee on payroll in the practice, you can connect the payroll service to your OWNER'S PAY account and rename it PAYROLL.

Depending on your salary, you may or may not have an additional amount allocated to *Owner's Pay*. If you are used to taking home more than the salary you and your accountant have decided on, you will still have an *Owner's Pay* allocation; it will just be smaller than before.

*Note: Reasonable compensation is beyond the scope of this book, but the goal is for the salary to be low enough to generate a tax savings for you, yet not so low that it's unreasonable. The amount should be in the ballpark of what you would pay someone to replace you. The tax savings from making an S corporation election come from the fact that you only pay Social Security and Medicare on the wages paid through payroll, not the rest of the profit generated by your business. You still pay federal and state tax on the entire amount, but not Social Security and Medicare.

IS AN S ELECTION RIGHT FOR YOUR LLC?
THERE IS NO ONE-SIZE-FITS-ALL RULE, SO I
RECOMMEND SPEAKING WITH AN ACCOUNTANT AS
THE PRACTICE APPROACHES $50,000-$100,000
IN PROFIT ON THE P&L REPORT (NOT THE PROFIT
BANK ACCOUNT). THEY CAN REVIEW YOUR SPECIFIC
TAX SITUATION AND EVALUATE WHETHER THIS
MAKES SENSE FOR YOU.

I have yet to encounter a situation where Profit First simply couldn't be implemented in a practice. If you find yourself thinking, *My situation is too complicated, Profit First could never work for me,* you are probably wrong. Chances are that someone else has been in a situation like yours and made it work, and it's likely that my team and I have encountered your situation and found a workaround that can work for you, too. If you feel like you're in over your head or are unsure where to start, join the Profit First for Therapists Facebook group to ask the group a question or email me at info@profitfirstfortherapists.com.

CHAPTER 9

Reverse-Engineer Your Practice to Live Your Best Life

IF YOU COULD HAVE EVERYTHING you've ever wanted, what would that look like? More travel? A new house? A second house? Fully funding your retirement account each year? Or would it be something less tangible, like never again having to worry when you swipe your debit or credit card at the store? Are you longing for that feeling deep down in your gut that lets you *know* you are financially secure?

Whatever your goal may be, I'd like for you to achieve it. Your business should serve you, and we can reverse-engineer your practice to give you everything you've ever wanted. It might take a little time, but it's out there, within your reach.

Financial success is rarely the result of luck alone. A study by Ramsey Solutions found that 93% of millionaires said they accumulated their wealth because they worked and saved, not because they had big salaries. Of the millionaires interviewed for the study, only 31% averaged a salary of over $100,000 per year over the course of their career, and one-third never made six figures in any single working year of their career.[6] You don't need a multimillion-dollar practice to live well, have a high impact in your community, and retire comfortably.

LIVING YOUR BEST LIFE

ONE OF THE GOALS OF Profit First is for you to pay yourself unapologetically. Too many practice owners put themselves last, and I don't want that for you. In this chapter, you'll figure out how much money you need to make to support yourself comfortably. Then we'll reverse-engineer your business to achieve it.

The Lifestyle Worksheet in Table 9.1 will show how much you currently spend and would like to spend in each area of your personal life. Take out a pen and paper or download the free Lifestyle Worksheet at www.profitfirstfortherapists.com/tools.

To complete the worksheet, enter a realistic estimate of what you currently spend in each category in the first column, Current $. In the Nice to Have $ column, I want you to dream a little and think about what it would take to live your best life.

	Current $	Nice to Have $
Mortgage or rent		
Car, insurance, and fuel		
Groceries		
Restaurants and meal delivery		
Utilities		
Clothing		
Gifts		
Activities (gym, kids' activities, etc.)		
Amazon (in my budget, Amazon has its own line item)		

	Current $	Nice to Have $
Insurance (life, home, umbrella, etc.)		
Daycare/child care (if applicable)		
Services (cleaning, landscaping, etc.)		
Travel		
Fun money		
Retirement and investment		
Education and student loans		
Donations		
(Additional category that applies to you)		
(Additional category that applies to you)		
TOTAL:		

Table 9.1: Lifestyle Worksheet

Are the totals a little surprising, or did you already have a sense of how much it takes to keep your household running each month?

HOW MUCH CAN YOUR PRACTICE PAY YOU?

NEXT, LET'S TALK ABOUT YOUR practice—specifically, your average fee per session. Don't go down the rabbit hole of your electronic health record (EHR) software trying to get exact numbers; for the purposes of this exercise, use an educated guess or simply divide last month's revenue by the number of sessions in the month.

Using the worksheet in Table 9.2 and some data you've already gathered, calculate the number of sessions needed each month to ensure that your practice can support your personal expenses.

1	Desired take-home pay (from your Lifestyle Worksheet)	
2	*Owner's Pay* CAP (from your Instant Assessment)	
3	Monthly average revenue (Desired take-home pay from row 1/ *Owner's Pay* CAP in row 2)	
4	Average fee per session	
5	Number of monthly sessions needed to meet revenue goal* (Monthly average revenue from row 3/Average fee per session from row 4)	

Table 9.2: Reverse-Engineer Your Practice Worksheet

*On average, one full-timffe clinician can see approximately one hundred sessions each month.

Step 1: In row 1, enter the total in the Current $ column from the Lifestyle Worksheet. This will be your desired take-home pay for the initial calculation.

For example, if your current need is $7,000 per month, enter that amount.

1	Desired take-home pay (from your Lifestyle Worksheet)	$7,000

Step 2: In row 2, enter the *Owner's Pay* CAP you calculated in the Instant Assessment. For this solo practice example, I am using a CAP of 48%.

1	Desired take-home pay (from your Lifestyle Worksheet)	$7,000
2	*Owner's Pay* CAP (from your Instant Assessment)	48%

Step 3: In row 3, divide row 1 by row 2. The calculation is $7,000/48% = $14,583. This means that if the *Owner's Pay* allocation is 48%, the practice needs to generate $14,583/month for the take-home pay to equal $7,000.

1	Desired take-home pay (from your Lifestyle Worksheet)	$7,000
2	*Owner's Pay* CAP (from your Instant Assessment)	48%
3	Monthly average revenue (Desired take-home pay from row 1/ *Owner's Pay* CAP in row 2)	$14,583

Step 4: In row 4, enter your average fee per session. In this example, I use $125/session.

1	Desired take-home pay (from your Lifestyle Worksheet)	$7,000
2	*Owner's Pay* CAP (from your Instant Assessment)	48%
3	Monthly average revenue (Desired take-home pay from row 1/ *Owner's Pay* CAP in row 2)	$14,583
4	Average fee per session	$125

Step 5: In row 5, divide row 3 by row 4. This shows us how many sessions per month it will take for the practice to generate the required revenue. If the *Owner's Pay* allocation is 48%, the practice needs 117 sessions per month to generate $7,000 in *Owner's Pay*.

1	Desired take-home pay (from your Lifestyle Worksheet)	$7,000
2	*Owner's Pay* CAP (from your Instant Assessment)	48%
3	Monthly average revenue (Desired take-home pay from row 1/ *Owner's Pay* CAP in row 2)	$14,583
4	Average fee per session	$125
5	Number of monthly sessions needed to meet revenue goal* (Monthly average revenue from row 3/Average fee per session from row 4)	117

Table 9.3: Reverse-Engineer Your Practice Example 1

There are three primary numbers that will affect how much your practice can pay you:

- Average fee per session
- Number of sessions
- *Payroll – Owner* or *Owner's Pay* allocation

We can use each of these numbers as "levers" to get to a desired result. Let's look at the same solo practice example, except we'll change the average fee per session in row 4 to $175 instead of $125.

1	Desired take-home pay (from your Lifestyle Worksheet)	$7,000
2	*Owner's Pay* CAP (from your Instant Assessment)	48%
3	Monthly average revenue (Desired take-home pay from row 1/ *Owner's Pay* CAP from row 2)	$14,583
4	Average fee per session	$175
5	Number of monthly sessions needed to meet revenue goal* (Monthly average revenue from row 3/Average fee per session from row 4)	83

Table 9.4: Reverse-Engineer Your Practice Example 2

Notice how row 5, the number of monthly sessions needed to meet revenue goal, is much lower with this new session rate.

Let's pull another "lever" to see how that changes the number of monthly sessions needed to meet the revenue goal. I'm using the same solo practice in the example in Table 9.5, except the *Owner's Pay* CAP is now 55% (instead of 48%, as in the previous example). At an average fee per session of $125, the number of monthly sessions needed to meet the revenue goal is 102 because the practice only needs to generate $12,727 to provide $7,000 in *Owner's Pay*. It's helpful to see how a shift in allocations can change the revenue a practice needs to generate.

1	Desired take-home pay (from your Lifestyle Worksheet)	$7,000
2	*Owner's Pay* CAP (from your Instant Assessment)	55%
3	Monthly average revenue (Desired take-home pay from row 1/ *Owner's Pay* CAP from row 2)	$12,727
4	Average fee per session	$125
5	Number of monthly sessions needed to meet revenue goal* (Monthly average revenue from row 3/Average fee per session from row 4)	102

Table 9.5: Reverse-Engineer Your Practice Example 3

You can do this exercise as many times as you'd like, pulling the various revenue "levers" in your practice. To see what it would take to live your best life, you can also do this exercise again with your Nice to Have $ total from the Lifestyle Worksheet.

Want to take it a step further? Try completing the worksheet based on a practice that is larger than yours. If the solo practice owner from our example is considering starting a group practice, for example, they can complete the worksheet with the small group TAPs to see how many total sessions would be needed to meet their *Owner's Pay* goal and hire accordingly.

WHERE DO WE GO FROM HERE?

EVEN IF MATH ISN'T YOUR thing, I hope you see how simple it can be to align your business with your personal financial goals.

But maybe you've just realized that what you truly want isn't achievable with the practice you currently have. Knowing is half the battle. If you feel like you've been trying to jam a square peg into a round hole, you now know why. There is only so much money you can squeeze out of your business at each stage of private practice. Now you can get to work figuring out what your practice needs to be to sustain your life.

After doing a similar exercise, group practice owner Brent realized that he had been taking "whatever was left" from his business. He'd been trying to live his ideal lifestyle, but without planning, he was coming up short. His spending was emotional rather than anchored in numbers. If he felt like he had money, he spent it. And when he did that, it meant that slow months— and tax time—were stressful. The amount that he was able to take from the business each month wasn't always enough to sustain his needs, but when he took whatever he wanted, the business suffered. His practice was doing well, but not quite well enough to generate the kind of income he wanted and consistently needed.

Brent knew that his haphazard system wasn't working. Because he wasn't willing to cut down on things like annual family trips or kids' activities, he needed to grow the business so it could give him the money he wanted. He reverse-engineered his practice and calculated that he'd need two additional full-time clinicians to be able to generate his desired *Owner's Pay*.

After he knew that, Brent started recruiting and marketing to fill the positions. Within a few months of hiring, he noticed that his lifestyle was being supported. His prior thinking had been that if he just made sure that the business was running smoothly, he would have enough money. But until he reverse-engineered his needs into his business and made it a priority to support his *Owner's Pay* allocation and pay himself first, it never quite worked. His business had to change to provide what he needed.

Brent loves his Profit First transfer day because he gets to pay himself and take care of his family. Now that he has been doing Profit First for years, he also enjoys paying taxes because he knows he has the funds to make the payment.

If your practice can't quite give you the cash you need today, I also suggest that you take another look at your personal expenses. Is there something that can be temporarily cut, or eliminated altogether? If you're accumulating personal debt just to sustain your lifestyle, you're going down a slippery slope. Consider making some changes.

I know that all these calculations can be a tad overwhelming, but each worksheet in this book will give you a better understanding of what's going on in your practice. Your financials are telling a story about your business, if you'll listen.

Ensuring that your practice can support you is just math, and when you look at the numbers, they aren't that scary. You are highly educated and capable, and at this point in the book, you have already learned the tools you need to get what you want out of your practice.

CHAPTER 10

Team Compensation for Group Practice: Pay Your Team Well While Keeping an Eye on Profit

THIS MIGHT BE A CONTROVERSIAL statement, but if your group practice is struggling financially, there's a good chance you are paying your team too much. I know it stings, but I've seen this issue come up enough times to know just how common it is.

I assure you that I say this from a place of kindness. I see your desire to give your team the very highest pay you think you can afford. Perhaps you've felt taken advantage of at an agency or working for someone else. I understand that you don't want to succumb to corporate greed. But your clients need your business to be profitable. I want every session and every clinician in your practice to be profitable.

Time and time again, my team onboards new clients with cash flow issues who have no idea where the problem is. When we dig into the numbers and realize that clinician compensation is making up too large a percentage of the monthly expenses, we ask about the compensation structure for the team and how it was decided upon. The most common answers: "I asked around in a therapist business owner group" or "I asked a friend how they are paying their team." Notice the question these practice owners didn't ask their colleagues: "Are you making a profit with that compensation structure?"

Lyle came to this realization after a few years in business: "I was just hiring people because I wanted to treat them really well, which is still my goal, but I finally realized that part of treating them really well means that I also have to make my business sustainable. So I *have* to think of the business when I make hiring decisions and make an offer to a potential new team member."

In other cases, we find that practice owners *did* have their eye on profit and just weren't sure if they could afford to pay more or offer additional perks. When Whitney Owens started working with my team, she shared that she had wanted to add health insurance and retirement benefits for years but was never quite sure if she could really afford it. After starting Profit First, she saw how much money was consistently left in her PAYROLL account and decided to take the plunge. She didn't have to make any adjustments to her CAPs because the allocations could already cover the expense. Because Whitney's practice is in a competitive area where it can be challenging to hire, having a highly engaged team is a distinct advantage. She added health insurance as a benefit and is hopeful that this addition will help her retain clinicians for years to come.

Setting a clinician compensation structure is a decision that can literally make or break a business, and yet there is seldom much time invested in getting it right. If you own a group practice, compensation is your largest monthly expense.

In this chapter, I'll present you with various compensation options. I'd like for you to think of it as a beautiful display case of options instead of a prescription. Choose what works for you and your practice and run the numbers.

There are five big decisions to make when it comes to compensation:

1. Will you hire contractors or employees?
2. How much will you pay your clinicians?
3. How will you structure their compensation?
4. Will payment occur at the time of service, or when the payment for service is received?
5. Will you offer any benefits to your team, now or in the future?

IF YOU'RE A SOLO PRACTICE OWNER OR AN EMPLOYEE THINKING OF GOING OUT ON YOUR OWN SOON, YOU MIGHT FEEL SOME ANGER TOWARD ME AS YOU READ THIS CHAPTER. HOW DARE I SAY YOU ARE (OR WERE) GETTING PAID TOO MUCH? IF YOU GO OUT ON YOUR OWN AND START A PRACTICE, YOU'LL MAKE YOUR FULL FEE, AND THAT'S WHAT YOU DESERVE. IF YOU HAVE PRIVATE PRACTICE AND BUSINESS OWNERSHIP IN YOUR HEART, I FULLY ENCOURAGE YOU TO GO FOR IT. BUT I WANT YOU TO BE CLEAR ON SOMETHING: NO ONE GETS TO KEEP THEIR FULL FEE.

WHEN YOU ARE A BUSINESS OWNER, YOUR
EXPENSES—LIKE SOFTWARE, RENT, COMPUTER,
ADVERTISING, ETC.—MUST NECESSARILY COME OUT
OF YOUR FULL FEE. YOU ALSO SPEND A SIGNIFICANT
AMOUNT OF TIME DOING THINGS YOU DIDN'T HAVE
TO DO WHEN YOU WORKED FOR SOMEONE ELSE,
LIKE BUILDING RELATIONSHIPS IN THE COMMUNITY,
BILLING, SCHEDULING, ANSWERING ALL INCOMING
INQUIRIES, TINKERING WITH YOUR WEBSITE, ETC.
YOU INVEST A SIGNIFICANT AMOUNT OF TIME IN
YOUR BUSINESS, AND THAT TOO MEANS THAT YOU
DO NOT GET YOUR FULL FEE.

CONTRACTORS VS. EMPLOYEES

IT CAN SEEM MUCH SIMPLER to hire a contractor, and a new group practice's first hire will often be a contractor. You can pay them by check or bank transfer, and there are no taxes to withhold. You should ask them for a W-9 before you pay them for the first time, and you'll need to make sure to issue a 1099 to your contractor at the end of the year. Why get a W-9 before the first payment? Years of experience have taught me that it's very easy to get a W-9 from someone who really wants to get paid, whereas the following January, when you're getting ready to issue 1099s, people aren't as keen on getting you what you need—especially if you haven't worked together in a few months.

Hiring employees means that you'll have to pay them through payroll. I recommend using a reputable company like Gusto, ADP, or Paychex to run payroll so that taxes are calculated correctly, wages are paid on time, and reports are filed as needed. Payroll is complex, and a small mistake can be costly, so it's worth spending a little money on a payroll software for the peace of mind that comes with compliance.

Some differences between contractors and employees are (note that this list is not intended as an exhaustive comparison):

Contractors	Employees
• Make their own hours	• Work hours set by employer
• Work how and when work they wish (owner cannot control how and when work is done, only what is done)	• Work according to employer's preferences for how and when work is done
• Are issued a 1099 at the end of the year	• Must be employees if they are provisionally licensed therapists (in most states)
• Have no tax withholding	
• Are considered self-employed	• Have federal and state tax withheld and remitted through payroll
• Typically pay their own liability/malpractice insurance	• Incur additional expenses for practice (Social Security and Medicare or FICA, federal and state unemployment and other insurance, workers' compensation, benefits (if applicable), and payroll processing fees/administrative time
• Have no benefit requirement	
• Have no unemployment insurance	
• Are sometimes excluded from workers' compensation	

Table 10.1 Contractors vs. Employees

A note on contractors vs. employees: Several states are working hard to make it difficult to hire contractors. When you're making the contractor vs. employee decision, I *highly* recommend that you consult with an employment attorney in your state. While hiring contractors can be simpler than hiring employees, consider the fact that you're never going to get in trouble for hiring employees, but you could get in trouble for hiring contractors.

I have noticed that for new group practice owners, hiring a full-time employee feels like much more pressure than hiring a part-time contractor. Doubt can creep in, with questions swirling in your head like, *What if there aren't enough clients for both of us?* or *What if I can't fill their caseload?* Overall, though, employees tend to generate far more revenue for your practice than contractors.

Gordon Brewer, M.Ed., LMFT, owner of Kingsport Counseling in Tennessee and host of The Practice of Therapy podcast, shared his contractor vs. employee experience with me: "When people shy away from having employees, I would say, really look at the numbers. My practice became much more profitable after I started hiring employees. They're happier, too, and I've had much better retention since then."

HOW MUCH CAN YOU PAY YOUR TEAM MEMBERS?

AS YOU NOTICED IN THE contractors vs. employees comparison, there are a few more compensation components to hiring an employee. Let's look at a few of them:

- **Gross wage:** The dollar amount you pay your clinician. If your clinician has a rate of $60/session, the gross wage is $60.

- **Payroll tax:** If you have employees, the employer is required to pay one half of FICA (Social Security and Medicare), federal unemployment, state unemployment, and, on occasion, other state-specific payroll taxes like disability or paid family leave. Depending on your state, this will amount to 8–10% of the gross wage, so for calculation purposes I like to use 10% to play it safe. (I like to overestimate expenses and underestimate income when forecasting.) Gross wage $60 + Payroll tax $6 = $66 cost to the practice.

- **Benefits:** Even if you don't plan to offer benefits today, do you plan to offer them eventually? If so, it's a good idea to build in some wiggle room from the very beginning. Benefits can easily add another 5–10% to the gross wage, sometimes more. Benefits might include health, dental, and vision insurance, retirement matching, paid time off, continuing education reimbursement, short-term and long-term disability, life insurance, etc. Gross wage $60 + Payroll tax $6 + Benefits $6 = $72 cost to the practice.

Do you see how this can quickly get out of hand?

Ideally, your licensed clinician costs—including wages, payroll tax, bonus, and benefits—should make up no more than 45–60% of the income *they* generate (you can expect to pay significantly less for pre-licensed clinicians because you'll need to provide supervision). That means the practice keeps 40–55% of the income to cover expenses like software, rent, marketing, intake, billing, leadership, and *profit*. There must be profit. This is where therapist guilt often rears its ugly head. You must get paid for the risk you take as a business owner.

That doesn't mean that you'll never be able to pay someone more than a 50% commission plus tax and benefits, but it does mean that if you have a team member at 60% commission plus additional benefit costs, you'll have to offset that with team members at a lower split to keep your average within the recommended range.

Here are my recommendations for compensation, from the TAPs table:

Target Allocation Percentages (TAPs)				
	Solo	Small Group	Medium Group	Large Group
Payroll – Therapists	0%	25–45%	45–60%	45–60%
Payroll – Admin	0–5%	0–5%	0–8%	4–7%
Payroll – Leadership	0%	0%	0%	3–5%

Table 10.2: Target Allocation Percentages (TAPs) for payroll

These allocations apply whether you have contractors or employees, the main difference being that if you have employees, you'll have to set their gross wage a little lower to compensate for the additional expense of payroll taxes and benefits. Contractors are responsible for paying their own payroll taxes and providing their own benefits (with a few exceptions), so they expect to get paid a little more than employees. These allocations also apply whether you pay clinicians at the time of service or when your practice receives payment.

CLINICIAN COMPENSATION MODELS

THERE ARE MANY WAYS TO compensate your team of contractors or employees, and each has pros and cons. Consult with your accountant and your attorney to decide which model will work best for you based on your state's laws.

Commission: This has been the most popular compensation model for many years, but I predict that commission-only positions will continue to decline over the next several years. In this model, your clinician gets a percentage of the revenue generated during each session. One of the reasons this structure is so popular is that it gives clinicians a direct incentive to see clients. The more a clinician works, the more money they can make.

Practice pro: The commission is only paid after the practice has been paid. This model can work for both employees and contractors. Minimum wage laws apply, so clinician employees should be paid at least minimum wage each pay period.

Practice con: It's increasingly difficult to recruit new team members for commission-only positions because of the uncertainty they pose to clinicians. Another drawback is that it's not as inclusive as other models because not all clinicians can afford to go a few weeks with only minimum wage. Clinicians requesting a raise expect an increase to their commission percentage, which will erode profit margins over time.

Clinician pro: The clinician receives an automatic raise every time an insurance reimbursement increases.

Clinician con: Clinicians may not get paid much for a few weeks after they start working at a practice. They are beholden to billers and insurance companies, over which they have no control.

Flat fee per session: For each session your clinicians see, they get a flat fee. This typically includes the note time for each session as well.

Practice pro: The same fee is paid to clinicians whether they see an insurance client or a private-pay client. When an insurance reimbursement goes up, the clinician fee stays the same. It is easy to pay them at the time of service, and the calculation for payroll is simple: Number of sessions x Flat fee = Compensation. This model can work for employees or contractors. There is no additional payment for administrative or note time besides team meetings.

Practice con: Not all EHRs make this information easy to get for payroll. It's often necessary to keep separate timesheets or session logs.

Clinician pro: The clinician knows exactly what to expect from each clinical hour worked. There is no variation between insurance panels and private-pay clients.

Clinician con: There is no potential increase in income for private-pay clients.

Hourly rate: In some states*, you're required to pay team members for each hour or portion of an hour worked, in which case an hourly rate can make sense. An hourly rate is very similar to a flat fee. However, you'll typically distinguish between clinical time and administrative time and pay for both For example, if your employee has a fifty-minute session and takes ten minutes between appointments to complete their notes, they'll get paid for fifty minutes at their clinical rate and ten minutes at their admin rate. This compensation structure is more complex and is most often used for employees (not contractors) and only when required by law. The admin rate must be at least the minimum wage in your state.

*State regulations are constantly changing. Please check with your employment attorney or Human Resources professional for guidance on rules in your state.

Practice pro: The practice has the ability to distinguish between clinical time and admin time and pay them at different rates.

Practice con: Admin time can creep up if not capped. Running payroll is more complex due to timekeeping requirements.

Clinician pro: Every hour worked is paid.

Clinician con: Additional timekeeping requirements.

Base plus commission: In some states, where a commission-only position isn't possible because of timing and hourly rate restrictions, base plus commission can be a good compromise. The clinician receives a base salary or hourly rate that is paid for each hour worked, typically around $15–$25/hour or at least minimum wage. In addition to the base pay, the clinician also receives a percentage of the income generated by their sessions at the time the income is received by the practice. This compensation model should only be used for employees, not contractors, because of its increased administrative burden. As an example, an employee might have a $20/hour rate with a 30% commission. They receive $20 for each hour worked when the service is rendered and receive an additional 30% commission when the practice receives the income.

> Practice pro: If a practice is required by the state where it is located to pay clinicians at the time of service, the base pay is significantly lower than a clinical hourly rate or flat fee. The up-front cost of hiring an employee is lower.

> Practice con: Complexity of timekeeping and running payroll.

> Clinician pro: The clinician receives a partial payment at the time the service is rendered and has the opportunity for increased commission based on private-pay clients or higher-paying insurance panels.

Clinician con: Only a portion of compensation is received at the time of service. The other portion is received at a later date. There can be a lack of clarity on compensation because of timing.

Salary: Salaried positions aren't as common, but they are increasing in popularity as clinicians look for more income stability from their employers. When clinicians are salaried, they receive the same amount each pay period, regardless of how many clients were seen or the income generated for the practice. This works well for very consistent clinicians who have strong client retention.

One thing that I find very interesting about the mental health industry is how often practice owners are willing to overlook the needs of the business for the benefit of the team. Don't get me wrong: Without a team, you cannot have a group practice, and taking care of your team will serve you well. But in any relationship, there is some give and take. If you give a salary to your team members, you must reserve the right to coach your clinicians if they are not meeting their session goals. The math has to make sense.

Take Michelle, for example, who is considering salaried positions for her team. She wants to base the salary on the twenty-five sessions per week that she expects her clinicians to do, even though most of her clinicians are consistently under the twenty-five-session goal and hover around an average of twenty-three to twenty-four sessions each week. For salaries to make financial sense for the practice, the clinicians will need to increase their average weekly sessions effective immediately and stay there. Past behavior is a very good indicator of future behavior, so why would Michelle make this choice? Additional risk to the practice is incurred when shifting employees from commissions to salaries because the practice's new fixed expenses (the salaries) remain the same no matter how much revenue is generated or what billing issues come up. I firmly believe that there must be a financial benefit to the practice, however small, in having salaried employees in exchange for the additional risk. I'd much rather see Michelle base her team's salary on twenty-two or twenty-three sessions per week and increase the salary later, after several months of consistently higher session counts.

Other health specialties, like physical therapy, often have salaried employees and expect thirty-seven to thirty-eight hours of client-facing time each week. Employees are scheduled for forty hours per week, often with some early and late days (as in the mental health field), and admin teams schedule them based on schedule maximization. When you hire salaried employees, you can and should monitor performance and keep your clinicians' schedules full.

Practice pro: Costs are capped and payroll is very simple to run. The practice can see an increased profit if the clinician's schedule is consistently full.

Practice con: Costs stay the same even if a clinician's session count is not up to expectation. Hiring new salaried team members is more expensive up front than any of the other compensation models, causing additional risk to the practice.

Clinician pro: The clinician knows exactly what to expect each pay period.

Clinician con: High-performing clinicians who are very consistent in their hours and client retention rates may prefer commission-only positions because they can increase their compensation by increasing their hours.

ADMINISTRATIVE COMPENSATION

THE TWO COMMON WAYS TO pay an administrative professional are hourly and on a salaried basis. It's always an option to start with hourly wages and move to a salary later. If your budget allows for it, I prefer hiring full-time employees instead of part-time ones. You'll get much more productivity, buy-in, and loyalty from one full-time employee than from two part-timers who also have other things going on.

If your budget only allows for part-time help, some help is usually better than no help. And if you plan to continue growing the practice, your part-time hire will ideally be someone who can grow with your practice. Just keep in mind that cobbling together a team of part-timers tends to be more difficult for the owner long-term than having a dedicated full-time staff.

The cost of hiring your admin or admin team will vary significantly depending on region. In some areas, you can find someone amazing for $15/hour without a problem. In metropolitan areas, you might spend closer to $30/hour to find someone comparable.

Hiring a virtual assistant (VA) company can also be a great option. While it tends to be slightly more expensive than hiring directly, your VA will have had some significant training already with the company you hire. They might already have experience with private practice or work with other, similar clients and be able to help you establish systems.

LEADERSHIP COMPENSATION

My team and I typically recommend the addition of a leadership level around the $800,000 – $1,000,000 annual revenue range. That tends to be the point where there are just too many team members for one owner to manage, and the owner needs help with the day-to-day management of the business so they can focus on their strengths. The team member added might be a clinical supervisor, clinical director, or site supervisor.

There are three common ways to compensate a leader: via an hourly leadership rate, a stipend (monthly or weekly), or a salary.

If you only need a few hours each week for a leadership role, an hourly rate or fixed stipend make sense. The rate should be higher than the team members' clinical rate so they are motivated to do the leadership work instead of seeing clients. It can also make sense to cap these hours to make sure they don't increase every week or pay period.

That might look like: 5 leadership hours/week x $75/hour = $375/week.

If you think your needs are minimal, you could also offer a flat fee stipend for each pay period, for example, a $500/pay period leadership stipend.

A stipend can also work well for other positions that require just a few hours here and there: intake assistance, onboarding of new clinicians, providing training for the team, etc. Hourly and stipend compensation are most common for site supervisors and clinical supervisors.

A leadership salary makes sense when the practice requires a significant number of leadership hours and is large enough to shoulder the weight of a large salary. A clinical director is a key member of the practice, and a salary is most common for this position. In most cases, leaders still carry their own client loads, but their clinical expectations are reduced to give them the time and space for their leadership duties.

For example, a leader who had previously been seeing twenty-five clients per week might drop to twenty clinical hours per week plus five to ten leadership hours.

Dr. David Goode-Cross, whom I mentioned in Chapter 6, planned to hire five new team members all at once. Up to that point, his practice had consisted of two to three clinicians other than himself, depending on the season. Before the hiring spree, we talked through the numbers and realized that, after the five new team members were on board, he'd be really close to needing a leadership team. David mentioned that he really didn't think he'd need a leadership team because his physical space would be full at that point and there wouldn't be any other positions open unless he planned to expand. After the five new team members were onboarded, though, he felt quite differently. Even though David hadn't been taking on new clients for some time, it had become too much to manage so many people and keep his own caseload.

In many cases, leaders rise from within instead of being new hires. A leader who already knows the team and the processes will be able to ramp up their work much faster than someone who is just learning the ropes of your business.

Because there is a decrease in revenue at the same time as an increase in costs, adding a salaried leadership role can be expensive—so my goal is for this position to be a break-even one. The leader might not contribute to overhead or profit, but ideally, they generate enough income to cover their salary, payroll tax, and benefits.

PAYMENT TIMING

ANOTHER BIG DECISION YOU'LL FACE when paying team members is timing. You have two options for commission and flat fee compensation: paying at the time of service or when the payment is received. This decision has a significant effect on cash flow for an insurance-based practice. For a private-pay practice that is consistent about collecting payments at the time of service, the impact of this decision will be negligible. The kicker here is that some states have regulations around how long the practice can wait to pay a team member after a service is rendered, so be sure to work with a human resource professional or an employment attorney to understand the requirements in your state. In most cases, you will need to pay at least minimum wage while you wait for insurance credentialing.

Let's look at the impact on an insurance-based practice. Paul shared his insurance experience with me: "Insurance can be tricky. It usually takes us between four weeks and six months to get a new clinician paneled. If there are any problems or issues, like the very first time you're trying to add a pre-licensed clinician—when things are a little bit different than the norm— it can take much longer to get paid." If you are committed to paying a clinician when the work is done, whether insurance has paid or not, a delay like the ones Paul has experienced can be costly for a practice.

Let's look at an example: You pay your team every other Friday. Your pay period is January 1–January 14, and your pay date is January 19. Your clinician, Jane, is a new hire who starts on January 2 and sees eighteen clients between January 1 and January 14. The insurance payment for Jane's sessions is received on February 20, roughly seven weeks later, because of a credentialing delay. If you pay Jane a flat fee of $65/session at the time of service, Jane will be paid $1,170 for the January 1–January 14 sessions on January 19, the next pay date. You pay Jane even though you haven't received a single dollar from insurance for the work she has done. If you pay at the time the insurance payment is received, Jane will be paid $1,170 on the pay date following the date the payment is received, or March 2 (two months later). Other than minimum wage (if required), you will not pay Jane until your practice has received a payment.

If you experience credentialing delays of several weeks, the up-front cost of a new hire paid at the time of service can be quite large. If Jane saw fifty-four clients over six weeks prior to your practice receiving an insurance payment, you would need enough cash to cover Jane's wages of $3,510 (54 x $65 = $3,510). For a large group practice, this might not be an issue; but for a new group practice, it can create a cash flow crunch. This is why many new group practice owners save up funds in an EXPANSION or FUTURE EMPLOYEE account prior to making a new hire.

Other issues can come up as well. Paul says, "Sometimes the provider manual with a particular insurance that you just got on hasn't been updated. So you submit claims and they are rejected. That can delay payment two to three more weeks, so a two- to three-month delay on payments is not unheard of. You're not exactly sure what's going on." When Paul wonders how he'll make payroll in the weeks after a new hire, he goes back to the buffer he's built in the PAYROLL account. Because he has planned for delays, Profit First allows him to anticipate and cover the increase in payroll so he knows he won't have to take out a loan or put expenses on a credit card. If the buffer in PAYROLL is not enough, he then turns to the EXPANSION account. The money is there because he's been planning strategically for each position. This has allowed his group practice to grow debt-free and give Paul and his family peace of mind.

WHAT IF YOU'RE PAYING TOO MUCH?

IF YOU'VE COME TO THE painful realization that you are paying some (or all) of your team members too much, know that you are not alone.

When I started working with Tammy, she was on the edge of burnout. Her group practice had grown quickly, and so had her clinical hours. It felt like she was on a hamster wheel and couldn't get off. She was seeing sixty clients each week and managing her team of six. Why so many clients? Her private-pay clients generated a significant amount of the practice revenue. If she slowed down or went on vacation, she had to contribute personal funds to the business to make payroll.

When we reviewed the numbers, it was clear that clinician compensation was an issue. Her team was paid between 75% and 85% of the revenue they generated, while Tammy worked harder than ever to cover the overhead for the entire practice because there wasn't enough money left to cover it after the clinicians were paid. The thing is, Tammy was almost out of personal funds to contribute, and she was terrified.

Most practice owners in the same situation are tempted to ramp things up: increase sessions, hire, get more clients. If you are losing money on each session, though, more clients will just make the situation worse.

In Tammy's case, that meant having a tough conversation with her team and changing her compensation model to one that was more sustainable (in case you're wondering, she offered her contractors a 60% commission). Four clinicians left, and her team of six went down to two. As scary as that was, the practice became profitable almost immediately. Had Tammy continued to hire without making any changes, it's likely that she eventually would have had to lay off the entire team and close the business.

Now that you have figured out what you *can* afford to pay, you might need to have a tough conversation with your existing team members. It's not going to be easy, and some clinicians will probably leave. But you probably can't keep doing this much longer, can you? Though your team feels like a family, do you want support that family? Do you want to give them your hard-earned money by seeing more clients so they can get paid more than you do? You've got to make a change, even if it's a slow one, or eventually you will run out of places to borrow money.

Here's what a conversation with your employee might sound like: "Amy, this is a really uncomfortable conversation for me. The practice has been struggling financially, and I've been doing a lot of work trying to figure out why and coming up with solutions. The biggest issue I have identified is that our current pay structure doesn't cover the practice's overhead expenses. As you know, we pay for office space, software, admin, marketing, etc., and it turns out we're losing money on each session right now. We need to make a change, or the practice will eventually have to close. I know this can't be easy to hear, but here's what I'd like to suggest…"

Don't you cringe just reading that? It's very painful, but 100% necessary if some of your clinicians generate negative profit for your practice.

PRO TIPS

BEFORE WE MOVE ON, I have a few more tips for you regarding compensation.

Tip #1: It should be clear to your team *how* they get paid. The simpler the structure, the better. If your team isn't crystal clear on how they get compensated, where the numbers come from, and exactly what you expect from them, you're doing a disservice to your business and your team. For example, if you have a complex, tiered system in which clinicians make a higher commission based on the number of clients they see, can your team tell where they currently stand? Is this something they can look up on their own, or do they need to reach out to you? Are no-shows included or not? What happens if they go on vacation?

Do you see where I'm going here? If your clinicians don't understand how the system works or where they stand, they won't produce the desired behavior.

Tip #2: It shouldn't take you days to run payroll each pay period. Is your system overcomplicated? How scalable is it? If it currently takes you one hour to run payroll for three employees, does that mean that it will take two hours to run payroll for six employees? Are you the only person who knows how to run payroll, meaning that no one could get paid if you had to take some unexpected time off? Do yourself a favor and keep the system simple. A simple, clear system will typically take less than two hours to calculate each pay period, no matter the size of your team.

Sometimes a compensation structure that seemed like a good idea early on turns out to be quite unwieldy as the practice scales. Kayla was in this situation when she first started working with my team. Her practice had grown quickly, and her commission structure had several pay bands that included many exceptions and "if this, then that" scenarios. It was taking her two full days to run payroll every other week. The system was so complex that no one on her team could help, and she had to time her vacations between pay dates. Another drawback of the complex payment system was that she was constantly answering questions from her employees about their paycheck calculations. There's just no need for things to be that complicated. A simple system will also make it easy for your team members to understand how their wages are calculated and allow them to check your work, should they want to.

Team compensation is the single largest expense for a group practice, yet a clear, simple system yields the best results. Don't be afraid to start slow to allow room for growth.

CHAPTER 11

Financial Bottlenecks: Reduce Expenses by Focusing on the Financial Issues with the Largest Impact

MOST SUMMERS, MY FAMILY AND I go to the beach in the Outer Banks. I love an evening walk when the sun has gone down and the cool ocean breeze has replaced the hot, sticky day. I'm happy to walk on my own, but I usually have at least one of my three kids ask to join me. My little one, Jackson, loves the feeling of the sand on his toes but doesn't like the darkness and the surprises nighttime might bring, so he carries a giant flashlight with him. As we walk quietly down the beach, he shines the light ahead of us, looking for creepy crawlers in the sand. These are mostly small crabs. He'd probably jump ten feet in the air if a crab happened to walk by his small foot in the dark, but because he's able to see them with his big flashlight, we can keep moving.

I want to shine my flashlight on some of the spending issues, or financial bottlenecks, that come up over and over again in private practice. If you know they're lurking in the dark and can see them coming, maybe they won't surprise you quite as much.

We have covered a lot of ground in this book, and you deserve a pat on the back for making it this far. You've seen the positive impact Profit First can have on your practice. If you've come to the realization that you need to adjust spending in your practice, this chapter will help to uncover your financial bottleneck and point you in the right direction so you can get it back on track.

When I think of a bottleneck, I think of a busy highway. My family and I live on the outskirts of Washington, DC, and there are usually lots of cars on the highway. On a Monday morning at five a.m., traffic is heavy, but everyone knows where they are going. It's not unusual to drive toward the city at sixty-five miles per hour (or more). But if one car slams on the brakes and the car behind it crashes into it, all the cars behind the crash have to slow waaay down. This is a lot like the systems in your practice: Your practice can grow quickly if all systems are growing at the same speed, but if one system slams on the brakes, all bets are off. You have to fix the bottleneck to get things moving again.

WHEN FIXED EXPENSES DON'T MAKE SENSE

FIXED EXPENSES ARE THINGS THAT don't change significantly from month to month. Rent, insurance, phone, and utilities are some of your fixed expenses. Other expenses, such as merchant fees and clinician pay (if your clinicians are paid hourly or on commission), are variable expenses because they increase as your practice grows.

Some expenses, such as admin and software, are more of a hybrid. It's likely that you'll always have a baseline for these expenses and, as your business grows, they will increase as well—just not proportionally to income.

One of my clients, Sheila, has a beautiful, large space in a desirable downtown neighborhood in a big city. It's bright and airy and just a gorgeous place to see clients. It has sixteen therapy rooms, a group room, and a welcoming reception area. The only problem? The rent is $18,000/month and she's only three years into a ten-year lease. Her insurance-based practice gets the same reimbursement as another therapist with a practice a few blocks away, who spends $2,800/month on rent for eight therapy rooms.

Sheila's challenge is, if the $18,000 fixed rent expense remains, there simply isn't enough money left at the end of the month no matter how many other expenses she cuts. To make the space work, she'd have to triple her number of clinicians and ensure that each room is in use twelve hours per day. Although that isn't impossible, it would certainly be challenging to pull off.

She is currently working with her attorney to break the lease, which is an extreme solution but will be very effective in turning things around. If that doesn't work, she's also considering alternatives like subleasing the space. To break even and stop losing money on a space with that price point, she'll need a monthly session count that's a little more than three times the current number. It's doable, but that kind of growth takes time. It also takes the right team, so it's not an overnight fix.

Ernie Schmidt, LCSW, owner of Palo Alto Therapy in California, business coach, and GroupPracticeSuccess.com mentor, experienced a different type of fixed expense bottleneck. He had just hired a new rock star admin to take the pressure off of his existing team of four admins. The team had been asking for additional help, so this was a win-win for everyone. Right around the admin's first day at the practice, two of Ernie's full-time clinicians gave their two-week notice. A few weeks later, he reached out to us because he'd just had the lowest-profit month in several years and wanted to understand what was going on in his practice. After reviewing the financial reports, I realized that he had encountered a fixed expense bottleneck in his large group practice. When he added an admin, his fixed expenses went up, while revenue declined due to the two departing therapists. The admin expense was disproportionately large, based on the current gross income of the practice, which tanked his profit that month. By the time we spoke, Ernie had already made an offer to replace one of the clinicians and was interviewing to replace the second one, so there was no need to let the new admin go. What a relief! Had the decline in revenue been permanent, the situation may have been entirely different.

Sometimes, to grow your business, you need to increase your fixed expenses to get to the next level. It's a natural part of growth and requires you to take a risk. We all learn by trial and error, and entrepreneurs are natural risk-takers. I'm asking you to keep an eye on your numbers: If the investment in your fixed expense is not paying off, it's time to ruthlessly cut the expense.

> THE FIX: In a group practice, if you really want to keep a fixed expense (team member, location, etc.), the easiest solution is to put the pedal to the metal to increase the number of sessions each month. That might mean holding your clinicians accountable for the number of weekly sessions they are expected to have, or you might need to hire. If you're in a situation like Ernie's, it would be silly to let someone go only to need them a few weeks later. On the other hand, if you're really not looking to increase revenue by hiring additional clinicians or seeing additional clients yourself, it's time to start cutting costs.
>
> In a solo practice, you have a finite amount of time and emotional energy each week. If you're unable or unwilling to see more clients, fixed expenses that are too high must simply be reduced.

OUT-OF-CONTROL PERSONAL EXPENSES

THIS ONE IS A LITTLE painful. One of the signs that personal expenses are your bottleneck is when the P&L report shows a profit but it feels like there isn't enough money in the business. Checks bounce, payroll is always a little tight, it's all-around stressful. When we dig in, what we often uncover is that the business is doing well, but the owner is taking out so much money for themselves—or worse yet, running personal expenses through the business—that there isn't enough money left to operate the practice.

Your business needs money like your body needs oxygen. If you deprive your practice of the money it needs to survive, you slowly choke it to death.

I get that it's easy to just book a personal flight on your business credit card (more miles, more credit available, better travel protection, we've heard it all), but this kind of decision makes it very difficult for your bookkeeper, accountant, or even *you* to remember what happened six months later.

Marcia was running all her personal expenses through the business. Personal rent, shopping trips, groceries, everything. My team and I knew so much about her life based on the transactions coming through the business bank account that we started to worry when the liquor store charges increased significantly. Marcia even paid for her new puppy and his cute puppy gear with a business credit card. At the end of the month, Marcia would ask us why she couldn't take a distribution. Why? Because she had already taken out all of the profit! It turns out that Marcia didn't want her spouse to see how much she was shopping, and *that's* why everything was going through the business. Luckily, Marcia and her spouse eventually went to couples' therapy and got honest about her personal spending, and her business has benefited from it.

You really shouldn't be running personal transactions through your business. It's a bad habit and it pierces the corporate veil, which is a fancy-schmancy way of saying that it reduces the legal protection you get from having a separate legal entity for your business. You and your business are separate entities and should have separate bank accounts. Transfer funds to your personal bank account and keep your personal spending there. Another consequence of comingling is that, under audit, all of your transactions could be reviewed to make sure you didn't let a personal transaction slip through. Just don't do it.

> **THE FIX:** Make regular transfers from the OWNER's PAY account to your personal account or pay yourself through payroll if your business is an S corporation. If you are using your business as a piggy bank because there isn't enough money in your personal bank account, go back to Chapter 9 to reverse-engineer your business to support your lifestyle.
>
> You still have to do the hard work of putting yourself on a budget in your personal life. If you know that you can reasonably take $5,000 from the business each month, you must make your personal expenses work within that amount. If you constantly borrow from the business or from your PROFIT account, Profit First won't work.

CLINICIAN PAY MIGHT NOT BE SUSTAINABLE

I'VE SEEN THE SAME SCENARIO play out time and time again. A therapist's solo practice is full and yet the phone hasn't stopped ringing. They decide it might be time to start a group practice and post an ad for a clinician position. The new group practice owner wants their new employee or contractor to feel valued and get paid well for the work they do.

They run the numbers, and it turns out that adding a clinician really won't increase costs much. No additional space is needed, and the group practice owner will continue to take all intake calls, handle scheduling, and do the billing. The only additional expenses will be a few software subscriptions and maybe a little advertising. No benefits will be offered either, so the group practice owner decides to offer the highest compensation possible for the position. This comes from a place of kindness, but it's not what's best for you, your practice, or your new employee.

On top of that, as group practices grow and mature, it's common to want to add benefits like health insurance, paid time off, continuing education reimbursement, and more. These are great recruiting tools, but they further erode your profit margin.

Clinician pay is one of the most common bottlenecks simply because it is typically the largest expense in a group practice. If this is the bottleneck, spending an hour on the phone to get your phone bill reduced by $20 will not move the needle toward profitability fast enough.

> **THE FIX:** This is always challenging. If this is your bottleneck, just know that I understand how hard it can feel. It can be fixed. First, I want you to go back to Chapter 10 and figure out what compensation you *can* afford to offer. If you're just getting started in group practice, I'd like for you to start with the end in mind. Where do you plan to be in five years? How many clinicians will you have? Will you be the clinical director, or will someone else be filling that role? How much admin support will you need? What benefits will you offer? Decide how much you can afford based on *that* scenario.
>
> After you've got that number figured out, your very next hire should be offered this new compensation package.

Next, you'll prepare to have a tough conversation with your existing team members, as outlined in Chapter 10 under the "What If You're Paying Too Much?" section.

Gordon Brewer, who shared his thoughts on hiring employees vs. contractors, went through this painful situation. After running the numbers to start Profit First, he knew that if he didn't make a change to his contractor compensation, the business couldn't be sustainable unless he worked harder and harder. He had just come to the painful realization that he was subsidizing his team members. They weren't contributing to overhead and profit, yet Gordon was putting in long hours just to be able to pay them. That's when the alarm bells went off. When he sat down to have difficult conversations with his contractors, he was mentally prepared to have to rebuild the practice from scratch. Luckily, one of Gordon's three contractors stayed on and is still happily working for Kingsport Counseling.

I imagine that this wasn't an easy process for Gordon, but he knew it was the right decision when he started making more profit with one team member than with three.

One of the issues that sometimes looks like a clinician pay bottleneck is a lax admin time or PTO policy. If your clinician payroll suddenly seems to be creeping up and you haven't made any significant changes, look at how payroll is being calculated. If your team is hourly and you offer an admin rate, is your team charging way more admin time than they are supposed to? For example, if someone on your team has been assigned to post on social media and given a five-hour/week budget to do it, you might see the number of hours slowly creep up to ten hours per week over several months. Your well-intentioned clinician might think that they are doing you a favor by doing more marketing, but if they have reduced their clinical hours at the same time, your practice could see a decline in income. An additional five hours each week at $40/hour can cost your practice an additional $9,600 each year, but more importantly, it can cost more than $30,000 in lost income. That really adds up!

As telehealth has become more mainstream, it's easier than ever for clinicians to go out on their own. That has caused a clinician crunch, making the hiring market even more competitive. No matter how difficult it might be to find a clinician, the numbers still have to make sense—or you're better off not hiring and will end up with more money in your pocket.

Profit First has given Angel Koenig a clear framework for compensation, which has helped tremendously with hiring. When a potential team member asks for significantly more than her practice is offering, Angel feels confident discussing compensation because she has clarity through her Profit First accounts. She knows exactly what she can afford based on facts, not feelings. That allows her to decide if she's able to offer a raise or if she's gone as far as she can go.

DEBT CAN DROWN YOUR PRACTICE

On paper (your P&L report) it looks like you're making good money, but your bank account says otherwise.

In the case of a debt bottleneck, we usually uncover that a significant amount of the profit is going to pay down debt. You see, debt payments aren't 100% deductible; only the interest portion of the payment is a deductible expense. When you receive a loan and the deposit hits your bank account, that amount is not taxable income, it's a loan. And when you pay the loan principal back in turn, the expense is not deductible. Let's use a simple example to illustrate this:

You take out a $50,000 loan. Your monthly payments are $3,000, with $2,500 applied to the principal and $500 applied to interest.

The outflow of cash in your business bank account is $3,000. However, the P&L will only reflect your $500 interest payment. So, while your P&L may show a profit of $6,000, you only have $3,500 in available cash after subtracting the principal payment ($6,000 profit – $2,500 principal payment = $3,500).

When the spiral of debt has started, it can be hard to get out of. The debt itself is often a symptom of another issue or bottleneck but quickly becomes a problem of its own. When you're ready to run payroll and there simply isn't enough money in the bank account to cover it, what do you do? In many cases, I see practice owners turn to the fastest loan they can get their hands on. That often ends up being the business version of a payday lender, a loan company that advances you funds based on accounts receivable or gives you a small loan with a huge up-front fee. There are no prepayment penalties because you pay 100% of the loan fee up front, which is often thousands of dollars. On the rare occasions when the interest accrues monthly, it's at an ultra-high rate (think loan-shark rates) and your monthly payment barely makes a dent in the principal.

Debt can also come in the form of credit cards. As soon as your business opened, you probably started getting dozens of credit card offers each month. It often makes sense to have a credit card for the business (remember, no business spending on your personal card and vice versa!) if you can pay it off in full each month. You know yourself: If you can use credit cards responsibly and pay them off each month, do it. If you know that you will charge things you can't afford, don't do it.

Group practice owner Ernesto Segismundo has mastered the art of maximizing credit card points. He travels extensively for his side business, Fylmit, and pays for the deductible business travel on credit cards. Then he uses the points to pay for his personal travel and vacations, which essentially gives him free vacations on a regular basis. Ernesto will be the first to say he wasn't able to do this a few years ago because managing his money was a constant struggle. He had a lot of "money stuff" to work through with his own therapist and knew his limits. At that time, credit cards were off the table. But now that he has a better relationship with money, he's able to see credit cards (and their points) as a game to be played rather than something that controls his life.

CREDIT CARD POINTS ARE NOT THE KEY TO WEALTH. DON'T BUY THINGS YOU CAN'T AFFORD JUST FOR THE CREDIT CARD POINTS. FOR EACH PURCHASE, YOUR CREDIT CARD WILL TYPICALLY GIVE YOU 1–2% OF YOUR PURCHASE AMOUNT IN POINTS. PLEASE DON'T SPEND $100 TO GET $1 IN POINTS.

I will cover debt at length in Chapter 12 and scaling in detail in Chapter 13, but I want to mention that it's absolutely possible to start *and* grow a practice without debt. It will take a little longer and require more planning, but it is possible.

THE FIX: If debt is your financial bottleneck, the first step is to stop adding to the debt. Profit First is an amazing tool to get your spending under control, and it can help you get out of debt. Continue to make your minimum credit card payments, but for the day-to-day operations of your business, you should only spend from your OpEx account debit card. Don't attempt to make large credit card payments at this point; the initial goal is for you to spend less than you make in order to stabilize your financial situation. When you know that your spending "fits" in your OpEx account, *then* you can really start to tackle and pay down debt. If this is your bottleneck, review Chapter 12 on paying off student loans and other debt.

GROWTH AND EXPANSION

GROWTH AND EXPANSION PROBABLY DON'T sound like financial bottlenecks, but they can be. During a time of growth, a practice owner gets pulled in several different directions. It's easy to skip steps, forget about the budget, and overspend, resulting in a cash flow crunch. I also find that practice owners typically underestimate the cost of growth.

Growth that is too fast or too aggressive can literally take down your business. Growth can also be life-changing, but it just has to be done right.

The most common expenses that cause a growing private practice to struggle are payroll and buildout costs.

Up-front payroll: There are two timing options for payroll: paying your team at the time the service is rendered or paying them when your practice is paid. Timing has a significant effect on the cash flow of the practice when you hire and is compounded when you hire multiple clinicians at the same time.

Buildouts: Buildouts are a mix of stress and fun. Most of my clients enjoy the process of working with an architect, picking out finishes, and shopping for light fixtures. In my experience, buildouts are almost always more expensive than initially planned. I have yet to see a buildout that comes in under or at the quoted cost, but I'm holding out hope that it does exist somewhere.

Opening a new location is a little bit like merging onto the highway. You hit the gas, increase your speed, and at some point, the merge lane ends and you just have to get on. I see the two to three months before a new location opens as the merge lane. There are lots of things vying for your attention: hiring new clinicians, starting the marketing engine, and getting systems and processes set up. All of these compete for your time along with questions from the contractor and your existing workload.

In a perfect world, your expenses will increase at the same time the practice income from your new space does. If not, those first few months—while you are paying rent but your income hasn't increased proportionally—can be rough.

THE FIX: Open an EXPANSION account several months prior to the planned growth and accumulate a pile of cash to fund the project. These funds may not cover 100% of the expenses related to the expansion, but it's always useful to have a stockpile of money.

FIX #2: The planning phase of any expansion is mission-critical. I'll go over the three phases of expansion in Chapter 13. Prepare a budget *before* the expansion. If you give yourself spending guidelines that are in line with the funds you have available, you can refer to the budget regularly. If you need to increase your spending in one area, you can try to decrease your spending in another. To prepare the budget, you should shop around so you can accurately estimate the costs.

After you've set a budget, stick to it! You'll probably need to make a few adjustments over time. If you keep yourself in check, you'll always spend less than you would if you weren't following the budget.

SHINY OBJECT SYNDROME

I THINK WE CAN ALL relate to having shiny object syndrome (SOS) about something in our lives. My husband, Mick, definitely gets SOS with board games. The pandemic had him spending way more time than ever on Kickstarter, and it seems like new board games are still being delivered to our house every few weeks.

Shiny object syndrome can manifest in a business, too. There is always *something* else out there, and it's easy to be dazzled by the shininess of something new—software, coaching programs, conferences, even professional services. When you know your business could be better, it's tempting to look for the new, exciting thing that will propel it to the next level. The saying "You have to spend money to make money" is true, but it can also be used as an excuse for spending. There are unintended consequences, too. For instance, it can be frustrating for your team when you're always adding new software to the stack; it can also create redundancy. I'd like you to assess the return on investment (ROI) of what you have purchased before you move on to the next thing.

What someone else in your circle of friends or colleagues is doing can also have a huge influence. When you're sitting around with a glass of wine, chatting with your business owner friends and hearing about how well they are doing, do you get the urge to replicate their processes? After all, if it's working for them, it should work for you too, right? It's easy to get caught in the comparison trap. When you're centered in where you want your business to go, identify the one or two advisors you know you can rely on so you can tune out everyone else.

The shiny object that caught Bianca's attention was a building. A close friend of hers, who is also a business owner, was in the process of buying a building for her business. Bianca came to us excitedly, wanting to see if she had enough cash to buy a building for her therapy practice as well.

My team and I often wonder if these shiny objects sometimes feel a little like status symbols to practice owners. We had a great discussion with Bianca, looked at her cash position and her financials, and determined that, based on her personal financial goals, it just wasn't the right time for her to buy a building. She had kids who were about to head off to college and planned to pay for their tuition in full while also contributing significant amounts to her retirement fund. If Bianca bought a building, she would have to reduce either her college or retirement savings, and that wasn't in line with her goals. We'll probably revisit this in a few years, but I'm confident that this was the right decision for Bianca.

In a lot of ways, it is harder to stay focused than jump toward the next shiny object. The constant distraction of something new can mean that nothing gets done well or completed. When you're scattered, it can be challenging for your team to follow along with your visionary brain and its new ideas. And as your team grows, your organization will naturally be less nimble, so making big, sweeping changes will get harder. If you're not sure which part of your business needs your attention the most, I highly recommend *Fix This Next for Healthcare Providers* by Kasey Compton.[7] Her methodology helps keep your eye on the area of your business that needs *you* the most. It will give you a more effective framework to propel your business forward and help you focus your efforts.

THE FIX: Establish a regular cadence at which you review business and personal expenses. At least twice each year, pull out your credit card and bank statements for the month and look at them line by line. If you're a fan of paying for a yearlong subscription all at once, you should look at the last six months of statements to make sure you don't miss anything.

As you go through each line, make notes for yourself or your team. Are you getting a return on investment (ROI) for each expense? If you are paying for ads, are you tracking their effectiveness? Are there monthly subscriptions you no longer use? Is your team spending way more than you realized on their company credit cards? Did you sign up for a few software "free trials" that asked for your credit card information and then forget all about the subsequent monthly fee? Identify transactions that were once shiny objects but are no longer being used and cancel your subscriptions. This is the time to cut back.

If an expense is adding value to your business, keep it.

Remember, by looking at the most common bottlenecks, we're shining a flashlight in the dark corners of your practice. The bottlenecks won't all apply to you, and they certainly won't all appear at the same time. When you see one, you'll know what to do.

CHAPTER 12

Paying off Student Loans and Other Debt

DEBT IS COMMON ENOUGH IN private practice that I decided to give the topic its own chapter. When you have significant debt in a business, it's a little bit like baking with one hand tied behind your back. You might succeed in making the delicious cookies you craved, but it's going to be way more difficult and there's a good chance you'll mess them up or drop the tray on the floor as you take it out of the oven. Your business needs cash to survive, and debt can suffocate your private practice dreams.

One of the many benefits of Profit First is that the percentage allocations automatically help you build a buffer for leaner times. If you receive an unusually large deposit at the end of the month, keep the same allocations even if the transfer amount is more than you need. If that period is followed by a leaner-than-usual beginning of the month, the previous period's overage will help see you through. If you're preparing for your worst month, your best month will feel like a walk in the park. Even if you are in significant debt, you'll need to build buffers into your Profit First accounts to make sure you don't have to go back into debt again. I'd rather see you pay off debt a little slower so that you don't have to take out another loan or max out a credit card again.

DEBT FREEZE

ONE OF THE GOALS AS you start Profit First is to stop adding to your debt immediately, and then pay it down as quickly as possible. I'm not mad at you if you had to take out a loan at some point, but the fact that you needed a loan tells me there's another issue in the practice that may be unresolved. With the Profit First accounts, the issue in your practice will come to light when you stop leaning on debt or credit to "bridge the gap."

Your first step is to stop adding debt to the balance. Start by making minimum payments on the loan each month, but don't add a single penny to the debt. You can't dig your way out of a hole by throwing the dirt back in.

I love a good TV hospital drama, and in every one I've ever watched, the ER doctors work to stop the bleeding before they do anything else. Before you make a plan to pay down debt, stop the bleeding (of cash) that is causing you to go into debt.

I already talked at length about clinician compensation in Chapter 10, but it deserves another mention. If you have a group practice, payroll is likely your single largest expense, so if your practice is accumulating debt, team compensation is probably at least partially responsible. In group practice, clinicians are the money makers, so each non-leadership clinician should help cover the practice overhead and generate a profit. Period. If you're in significant debt and a clinician costs you more money than they generate, they simply cannot stay on your team. The math doesn't work.

Remember Tammy, my client who was paying her team 75–85% of the revenue they generated? Tammy had been working harder than ever to cover the overhead for the entire practice because there wasn't enough money left after her clinicians were paid to cover it. She had been contributing personal funds to the business continuously to try to keep it afloat, but was almost out of those personal funds to reinvest in the business, and she was terrified. Her debt wasn't to a lender, but to herself, so the first thing she had to do was stop the bleeding. She made some tough decisions and changed her compensation model. Tammy ended up with a smaller practice, but one that was profitable. Had Tammy continued without making any changes, it's likely that the business would have failed. Tammy successfully stopped the bleeding.

REDUCE EXPENSES TO INCREASE AVAILABLE CASH

Pull out the last three to six months' bank and credit card statements. If you use QuickBooks Online, you can also run a P&L detail report for the last few months to see every single expense in the business. Review the document line by line and highlight anything that can be cut, canceled, or stopped.

You can also call your credit card company and request that they issue you a new credit card with a new number. As a "courtesy," the company will sometimes transfer over your automatic monthly charges. Ask them not to do that. Having all of the charges transfer over to the new card won't help. As payments are declined, you will start getting emails and calls from vendors asking for a new payment method. Now you're in the driver's seat as far as which expenses you keep or not. I'm not suggesting that you shouldn't pay what you legally owe a vendor if you have a contract; this strategy is mostly for all the subscriptions you didn't really need but never got around to canceling. I simply want you to take back control of your bank account and credit cards.

After the initial round of expense elimination, go through the list of expenses again. Is there anything that could be substituted with a lower-cost alternative? With software especially, there are always new options out there. Does one of your subscriptions include a new feature that could eliminate another subscription? If you don't know where to start, there are some trustworthy organizations that can help you. My friends at Person-Centered Tech are great at finding software savings while keeping you HIPAA-compliant.

PAYING DOWN THE DEBT

ONE WAY TO MAKE A significant dent in debt is by allocating a line item to debt payments in your Profit First TAPs, as mentioned in Chapter 8.

Another way to get aggressive about paying down debt is by using most of the quarterly profit distribution to make large principal payments. At the end of each quarter, you'll typically take half the funds in your PROFIT account and transfer them to your personal account. When the business has debt, though, we modify this a little. I want you to keep a small part of that distribution, around 5–10% of the amount, to do something fun and reward yourself for your hard work. The remainder of the funds will go directly toward paying down debt.

Let's look at an example. If Amanda has a balance of $5,000 in her PROFIT account at the end of the quarter, $2,500 will stay in the PROFIT account and she will have $2,500 to work with for her reward and debt payment. She can spend $250 on a fancy dinner, while $2,250 will go directly toward paying down the principal balance of her debt.

Darla Sinclair purchased a building for her practice, The Body Mind Center, in 2019. She financed the commercial property with both a traditional mortgage and a personal loan with a five-year term. Darla used her quarterly profit distribution to reduce the personal loan rapidly and paid it off two years ahead of schedule. She didn't want the personal loan hanging over her head any longer than necessary.

TIP: WHEN YOU PAY DOWN DEBT, MAKE SURE YOUR ADDITIONAL PAYMENTS ARE APPLIED TO THE DEBT PRINCIPAL, NOT AS AN ADVANCE PAYMENT. THE ENTIRE PAYMENT SHOULD REDUCE THE BALANCE OF THE LOAN SO YOU DON'T END UP PAYING INTEREST IN ADVANCE.

REFINANCING YOUR DEBT

REFINANCING DEBT CAN HELP LOWER your interest rate, but it doesn't fix a spending problem. If you're able to get a lower rate or better terms by refinancing, it's worth considering *only* if you also change your financial habits. If you keep spending in exactly the same way, refinancing will only increase your total debt by putting it out of sight and out of mind. All debt is not created equal, though, so if you are able to refinance high-interest or predatory loans with high fees with a fixed interest rate loan, it can give your practice the breathing room it needs.

Elias was in this situation. A series of generous raises for his team caused him to get his first loan with a broker named Bob. I have never met Bob, but I just imagine him sitting at his desk, rubbing his hands in delight as another struggling business owner calls him for a loan. Every time someone signs on the dotted line for a loan they can't afford out of desperation, without having even read the fine print, I'm guessing that Bob makes a handsome commission. Elias took out a loan with a $10,000 up-front fee, and when he ran out of money just one month later, Bob refinanced that loan into a larger amount with another $10,000 fee and a twelve-month payment term. In just two months, Elias accrued $20,000 in loan fees and was about to run out of money again. His line of credit was already maxed out and the bank was unwilling to increase it. I could hear the fear in Elias's voice when we talked—fear for his family, his business, and his team.

Luckily, this story has a happy ending, thanks in part to a personal, fixed rate home equity loan. (In case you're wondering,

Bob wasn't involved with that loan.) A personal loan is certainly not my first choice when it comes to refinancing business debt, but Elias had personally guaranteed the loans he received through Bob, so he was responsible for the loan balances even if his business failed. When Elias got a loan at a low fixed rate, he was finally able to pay off the high-interest loans. Even with the influx of money, getting out of debt wasn't a fast or simple process. My team and I were committed to making sure that Elias was never in the position to need a last-minute loan again, so that meant building up reserves while paying down the debt. I'm happy to report that Elias has implemented Profit First in his practice and is paying down the loan each month.

GET AGGRESSIVE WITH YOUR STUDENT LOANS

It's not unusual for therapists to have $100,000 or more in student loans. That burden can be heavy when you have other financial responsibilities. After all the business debt has been paid off, turn your attention to your student loans as quickly as possible. Ideally, your monthly *Owner's Pay* transfers will be large enough to also make a dent in your student loans.

Kam was proud to have held allocations steady during the uncertainty of the pandemic. Their large student loans were in forbearance for several months, with no interest accruing and no payments due. During that time, Kam still made payments to aggressively reduce the principal of the loan. Because they had accumulated a good enough buffer in the Payroll and Tax accounts, they also decided to shift 0.5% from each account to OWNER'S PAY to cover additional principal payments each month. Half a percentage point sounds small, but it can still have a large impact over time.

Just as with business debt, I recommend that you use your profit distribution to pay down the balance. However, because student loans are typically quite large, my payoff formula for them is a little different. At the end of each quarter, take half the funds in your PROFIT account and transfer them to your personal account. In this case, I want you to keep half of that distribution to do something fun as a reward for your hard work. The remainder of the funds will go directly toward paying down your student loans. This is a less aggressive approach simply because it's a long game. Paying down tens of thousands of dollars in loans can take years, and it's challenging to stay patient for that long.

I've noticed that after our clients pay off their student loans, a visible shift happens in them as business owners. They take more risks and seem more confident because of their financial stability.

Unless you're at the finish line of a student loan forgiveness program, I want you to make so much money in your practice that you won't qualify for student loan forgiveness. Keeping your business small just to qualify for forgiveness in more than five years just doesn't make sense.

There is a common misconception that it's no big deal to keep a student loan around as long as possible because you can deduct the student loan interest on your personal tax return. Although this is partially true, there's a good chance that, as a private practice owner, you (and your household) will soon be making too much money to even qualify for the student loan interest deduction.[8] The deduction phases out, which means that beyond a certain income threshold (which the IRS changes annually), you won't be able to deduct your student loan interest at all. Time to kick the loans to the curb.

DEBT ACTION PLAN:

1. STOP THE BLEED.

2. REDUCE EXPENSES.

3. PAY DOWN DEBT.

4. PAY OFF DEBT AND CELEBRATE!

5. RECALCULATE ALLOCATIONS.

If a business is drowning in debt, it's hard to stay focused on profitability. It's easy to wonder, *What's the point?* I get it. But I would argue that if you have debt, you need profit even more. The solution to this problem is for your business to be as profitable as possible so that you can pay off the debt.

CHAPTER 13

Scale Your Practice Effectively

MENTAL HEALTH IS A FIELD with a low cost of entry compared to other medical professions. A basic website, a few software subscriptions, a liability insurance policy, and a computer are often enough to get started. While the first few months of any business will rarely be highly profitable, a private practice should start turning a profit quickly.

Most practice owners I speak with have the goal of growing their practice, either right now or at some point in the future. Although a large practice can bring in higher revenue, that isn't guaranteed to generate more profit for you, the owner. Business owners are optimists at heart, so they tend to think, *If I can just hire one more person, or get one more referral partner, or make things more efficient, I will finally make a profit.* The reality is, growing an unprofitable practice will only amplify your money problems, not fix them. Your business must become profitable *before* you can successfully scale a practice.

When your practice grows rapidly, one of the biggest dangers it faces is running out of cash. Many large, seemingly unstoppable businesses have failed because of a lack of funds. In fact, according to a study by U.S. Bank, 82% of businesses that fail, do so because of poor cash flow management.[9]

As each payroll gets bigger and bigger, and as you and your team plug systems holes with more software and more people, things can quickly get out of control. In my experience, it's not uncommon for a practice to have its lowest profit month just a few months after the highest gross income month. It's an emotional roller coaster of, "First time over $100,000/month, woohoo!" Followed by, "Oh, crap, now we have a negative profit."

Growth is good, but running out of cash is not. One of the many ways Profit First will help your growth is by anchoring your decisions in fact.

During the growth period, your Profit First allocations will likely change often, and that's normal. With so much change going on in your business, you won't be able to stay on financial autopilot; you'll need to keep a close eye on the money flowing in and out of the practice. This is especially true if you are cash-flowing your expansion project (in part or in full), which means that you are relying on current profit to pay for expansion expenses instead of having a big pile of cash saved up in advance.

If you're struggling to make ends meet with one location, two will not make it easier. If you're struggling to make payroll with five employees, ten employees will only add pressure to the cash flow crunch. Expansion will not magically make your practice more profitable; in fact, it will add stress to the systems that are already in place and their problems. Growth is almost always more expensive than planned.

The most successful expansions I have seen have followed a three-step process that starts with, and spends quite a bit of time in, the planning phase.

Phase 1: Planning. During this phase, you save for the expansion, consider options, interview potential employees, or even visit new office space. This phase can last for a few weeks to a few years.

Phase 2: Action. This is the exhausting, expensive three- to twelve-month period of action and hard work, the growth spurt during which profit tends to be leaner. You might be tempted to second-guess your decision to scale during this action-packed phase.

Phase 3: The New Normal. During this phase, your financials start to stabilize and you find your footing as the owner of a larger business. You might still be hiring, advertising, and adjusting, but you've implemented processes and are measuring what matters. Your profit (finally) catches up. It can take up to one year after expansion for that to happen, so enjoy the fruits of your labor.

The planning phase is by far the most important, but it's also the easiest one to skip when a business owner gets excited and jumps right in. A failure to plan is a plan to fail, so let's look at each phase more closely.

This chapter may not be as relevant for you if you're a solo practice owner who doesn't intend to grow, but if there's a possibility you might expand at some point, I encourage you to continue reading. I have met quite a few *accidental* group practice owners over the years.

PHASE 1: PLANNING EXPANSION

AN EXPANSION ACCOUNT IS THE simplest path to stress-free business growth. As I mentioned in Chapter 8, you can open that additional bank account and start allocating a percentage to cover all of the onetime costs associated with the expansion. Here's a list of expenses to consider:

Adding a Location: Costs will include first and last month's rent, furniture, buildout and leasehold improvement, a grand opening event, legal fees to review the lease, additional admin needs, recruiting costs, etc.

Adding Benefits: Costs will typically include the first monthly payment, sometimes before you have started your team members' deductions. Costs will vary based on the size of your team and which type of benefit you are adding, but adding benefits can easily cost from a few hundred to a few thousand dollars per person annually.

Adding Clinical Staff: You might incur significant costs for recruiting, interviewing, and training pay, and you'll want to be prepared for the first few weeks of a team member's employment with you, especially if you'll be paying them before the practice receives any insurance payments for their work. You may not need an EXPANSION account if you already have a large team and are adding one team member at a time with a few months in between. But if you plan to add three or more clinicians at once, having some cash saved up will reduce your stress level.

Adding Admin or Leadership Staff: These key positions are important in any group practice, even though they do not generate revenue directly. Sustainability is key here: You want to make sure that you can afford to pay this new wage for the next few weeks, but also long-term. Adding an overhead position will typically lead to more growth, but it's not a linear path to more revenue in the practice. You'll want to have, at minimum, two to six weeks' worth of the new salary saved up.

When Kate Fish, whom I mentioned in Chapter 5, was preparing to add a location to her practice, she felt nervous. She said, "I've never spent so much money on something before as I did on the buildout of my new office. I had no concept of how expensive it would truly be. It's like when you buy your first car—you have no concept of how much money you need."

The project was months in the making, and Kate worked with my team to budget and save for the big move. She had been allocating funds to her EXPANSION bank account for some time and was planning to cash-flow the rest of the cost with continued allocations to the account.

"When you're doing a buildout for a business, as someone who is a therapist and not in commercial real estate, I don't know how much these things go for," Kate shared with me. "But I can put the buildout into context and know that if it's this percentage of my income, that feels safe. It's not going to take away from other things because I'm still allocating enough to our operational costs." She had a plan, a budget, and a clear path to funding her expansion without putting the rest of her business at risk.

MANAGING YOUR EXPECTATIONS DURING THE PLANNING AND ACTION PHASE

LET'S BE REALISTIC. WHILE YOU are saving for an expansion, or during the period of growth, you will likely have to reduce your *Profit* allocation or make cuts in other areas. That's completely okay, but I want you to be prepared for it. It's extremely rare for a practice to have so much extra cash in OPEX that no changes are necessary. Your allocations must add up to 100% no matter what, and Profit First won't make money magically appear in your accounts. There are some sacrifices to be made now for the future reward your expansion will bring.

If you're able, plan for a specific dollar amount that you need to take home during the time of expansion. Is it realistic? Will the allocation to your PAYROLL – OWNER or OWNER'S PAY account still cover your needs at home? Expansion cannot come at the cost of your personal life; if it means you'll need to put groceries on credit cards for six months, you shouldn't do it. If you're able to plan on this amount and not much more, will you have enough money for yourself and your family? Will you be able to cover once-per-year expenses like home insurance and holiday gifts? Knowing exactly what to expect will help your family support you during this time.

That's why the planning phase is also a great time to make sure the expansion makes financial sense. Let's look at a few examples.

EXPANDING OR ADDING SPACE

BASED THE TERMS OF THE lease, do you have enough money to cover expenses until the day the space starts generating revenue? If the space needs significant changes to accommodate your practice, a buildout can take a few months to complete, and you may already be paying rent during that time.

If you are looking at a larger or additional space, can the space allow for enough sessions to support the additional cost while keeping your expense allocations in line? If your TAP is to spend no more than 5% of your income on rent, a space with $1,000/month rent must be able to generate $20,000/month in revenue. If your average session fee is $125, that means you'll have to schedule 160 sessions each month. If the space has one therapy room, that equates to forty sessions each week or eight per day. It can be challenging to keep space that full, but it's not impossible. If there are two therapy rooms, it will only take four sessions per day to meet your revenue goals, which is much easier to achieve.

It's easy to get swept up in the excitement of adding a new location. But it's important to keep your head on your shoulders and consider the true cost of a buildout.

Scenario 1: The landlord offers you a buildout allowance based on you signing a lease for a specific term, typically at least three years. Get a quote to see if the allowance will cover your buildout needs. Many landlords will give you an estimate, even though they are not contractors.

Scenario 2: In some cases, the landlord will offer the space "as is" and the tenant is responsible for any changes to the space. When this is the case, give some thought to what you'd like to do with the space and ask the landlord for permission to bring in some contractors (preferably two or three) to get quotes. Because you're responsible for coming up with the cash, you should know how much you need before you sign the lease. You'll typically need to pay the contractor a deposit up front and then, depending on the size of the project, make milestone payments or a final payment at the end of the project. If changes are made during the construction, the contractor should present you with a change order showing the cost difference and may ask for additional funds at that time or include the changes on the final invoice.

Maureen Werrbach, who shared her experience with therapist guilt in Chapter 1, has a smart take on negotiating the lease on a new location. She says, "My goal is to negotiate a few free months up front so that by the time I have to start paying the lease, the buildout is complete and the space has started generating revenue." She also gives herself a strict furniture and décor budget of $2,000 per therapy room. Instead of an EXPANSION account, Maureen builds a buffer in her OpEx account to pay for the furniture. If she's looking at a space with ten therapy rooms, she knows she'll need $20,000 for furniture plus a few thousand for the waiting room and kitchen, so she waits to have at least an extra $25,000 in OpEx. This is a great way to manage cash flow during the expansion and helps reduce the up-front cost of moving into a new space.

Kasey Compton, who has automated her practice as much as possible, now has seven locations and counting. She allocates funds to her EXPANSION account every time she makes her transfers, and because she's opened so many offices, she knows exactly how much money she needs saved to open a new location. When the balance of the account reaches the threshold, it's time to expand. There is no guessing; her EXPANSION account tells her when it's time to grow the business.

Your strategy for expansion might look different from the examples I just shared, but what Maureen and Kasey have in common is that they know how they will pay for an expansion before they start the growth process.

The buildout is one thing, but there are lots of other expenses that come up when moving into a new space—internet installation, moving fees, initial supply purchases, and the largest of them all: furniture. You'll need couches, coffee tables, chairs, lamps, wall décor and more to make the space warm and welcoming to your clients.

Most of our clients absolutely love this phase of opening a new location. They scour local stores for the best values, deciding which items they'll spend top dollar on (typically the therapist chairs) and when to choose more affordable options.

During the initial budgeting phase, furnishings are usually an afterthought. That's a mistake because they do add up to a significant amount of money that you'll need to come up with.

ADDING AN OVERHEAD POSITION

Admin positions are indirect revenue generators. Although your admin won't provide therapy, they will keep the wheels of your practice turning with mission-critical tasks like scheduling, verifying benefits, submitting insurance claims, processing payments, and more. A clinical director and site supervisor will help manage the team, maintain a high quality of care, and keep their fingers on the pulse of staff morale. If you're stretched thin, adding an overhead position will also help the practice grow while giving you back some quality of life.

Just because a position is important, though, doesn't mean that you have an unlimited budget for it. As you prepare for this hire, you'll want to determine if the practice has enough income to support the position.

The planning process for adding overhead positions is very similar to evaluating the addition of another location. If your goal admin allocation is 5%, to spend $5,000/month on admin, your practice must generate $100,000/month. If your allocation is 7%, you'll have $7,000 to "spend" at the same monthly revenue. You can split the amount as you see fit. It could pay one full-time team member or multiple team members; the decision is up to you. If you decide to spend a little more than that, consider what other allocation you'll reduce to get there.

ADDING NEW CLINICAL HIRES

Based on your compensation structure, do you have enough money to support the initial cost of adding new clinical staff? As we reviewed in detail in Chapter 10, if you pay your new clinician at the time the service is rendered, you may end up paying an employee before you have received any money from insurance. To avoid "How am I going to pay this person?" stress, estimate how much money you'll need before making an offer. Ideally, you'll have that amount in your Expansion or Payroll account, ready to be used if you need it.

ADDING A SIDE BUSINESS OR REVENUE STREAM

It's common for practice owners to want to add passive income or a side gig to their practice. There are so many options for this, like coaching, retreats, conferences, courses, weekend intensives, and more. The initial investment needed to add another income stream will vary. In many cases, the dollar amount will be minimal but your time investment will be significant, which can in turn reduce your practice income if it requires you to reduce your clinical hours. A little planning goes a long way.

Cathy Ranieri credits Profit First for giving her the confidence to start a consulting business, Cathy Ranieri Consulting, LLC, in addition to her private practice. She is passionate about walking alongside therapists who want to start their own solo practices, and her work as a consultant allows her to share best practices based on the lessons she's learned along the way.

Cathy finds the structure of Profit First reassuring. When she started implementing Profit First with Heidi from my team, she was already on the right track but didn't know it. She said, "Without Profit First, I don't know that I would have had the space and vision to create a consulting business on the side. If I was still unsure of where I stand financially, I don't think I would have had the emotional space available to think strategically about a new project like that. I can have the space for visionary work and know that there is enough money to keep my practice going."

This also created a shift for Cathy from a scarcity mindset to an abundance mindset. Prior to Profit First, she was hyper-focused on keeping expenses as low as possible. Now she can look at her OpEx account and decide how much she wants to meaningfully spend. She focuses on value-added services, or products that will increase her revenue or protect her time, instead of keeping expenses as low as possible (to the possible detriment of other areas of her life).

Because her coaching business didn't require a significant investment up front, Cathy is focused on building infrastructure so she can scale when she is ready. As a solo practice owner herself, she knows how much revenue she must generate from her clinical work to support her personal life. She has clarity around how much time she can spend each week on building out her coaching program, with the goal of splitting her time equally between therapy and coaching in the near future.

TAKE A LEAP OF FAITH

In planning expansion or growth, there is always a point that requires a leap of faith. You may never be completely prepared or ready for the new adventure that awaits you, but when the data supports your decision, the leap of faith will be easier.

When you use an Expansion account, the numbers tell you if you're ready to expand or not. Do you always have to borrow against the account to make payroll? You're not ready. Is it challenging to allocate a few percentage points to the account? You're not ready. Is the balance growing steadily, while you have a little more money than you need? You're probably ready.

If the numbers are telling you that your plan won't work, listen to them and then adjust your plan. That might mean giving yourself more time, looking for a cheaper space, or just getting creative. For example, if your revenue is not where it needs to be to support a new hire, you can still decide to take a leap of faith. After all, this is your business, and you are in the driver's seat. With the data in hand, you know that you'll have to get creative to make sure there is enough money in the bank to pay your new team member. Will you (temporarily) reduce your *Profit* allocation to make it work? Or get cracking on accounts receivable to quickly get cash in the door? Just because the potential new hire is amazing doesn't mean that math no longer applies. By planning ahead, you can set yourself and your new hire up for success.

PHASE 2: ACTION

AFTER YOU'VE MADE THE DECISION to expand, the project will almost always be more expensive than planned. Even the best-laid plans can have a wrench thrown into them. For example:

- Building materials increase in price and the contractor springs a surprise bill on you.
- The space is darker than you had anticipated, and you need to buy twenty additional lamps.
- The sink in the break room isn't connected to a water line, and you need to pay for that yourself. (This happened to one of my clients. What is the point of a sink that isn't connected to a water line?)
- There are delays in insurance reimbursement for your new hire, and you must wait over six weeks before their first payment comes through.

When you're in the action phase, you've made the plan and have a budget. Now, it's time to get things done. Remember, a budget is permission to spend. You've allocated funds to various categories, so don't feel guilty about buying the things you need.

In this phase, it's not uncommon for you as the owner to take home a little less money than you have previously, which can be unnerving. Even though the situation is temporary, it can make you second guess your decision to scale. Questions like *Will it be worth it?* or *What have I done?!* might be swirling around in your head, and that is a normal part of the process.

It can be helpful to revisit the plan at this point, just to remind yourself that everything is on track.

Kristen Breese, whom I mentioned in Chapter 7, opened her fourth location a few months ago. The expansion was planned, funds were allocated, and the numbers made sense. The competition in the area is minimal, the building is easily accessible from several major roads, and there was almost nothing to do to the interior of the space for it to house seven therapy offices. Still, the expansion has been a drain on financial resources, and Kristen's *Profit* and *Tax* allocations are still lower than they were before the new office opened. That's due in part to higher than usual turnover among the team during the same period. Even though the practice has been hiring steadily to fill the new space, due to the team attrition, the hiring hasn't increased the session count or revenue significantly—yet.

With a steady reminder from her accounting team that this is all part of the plan, Kristen is confident that revenue and profit will increase any day now. She knows exactly how many clinicians she needs and what the weekly and monthly session counts need to be for the new space to become profitable. One way that Kristen has been very intentional about staying on-budget is by shopping online resale sites to furnish her new space. She's purchased everything from couches to coffee tables secondhand, which allowed her to splurge on a few nice things for each office.

The action phase typically brings a few surprise challenges, and it can feel a little like playing a game of Whac-A-Mole. At some point, you might feel tired and worn down from being so busy. It's a normal part of the process. Review your plan and keep going. You've got this.

GROWING WITHOUT DEBT

I AM OFTEN ASKED IF it's possible to scale a practice without debt, and I'm happy to report that it is absolutely possible. In fact, most of the growth stories in this chapter are ones in which the practice owner didn't borrow a single penny.

Growing your practice at the speed of cash isn't as exciting as using a loan to make big moves, but it reduces your risk significantly. When you save up for growth with an EXPANSION account, that means your cash flow is good enough to support your practice expenses *and* contribute to a separate account. That puts your business in a really good position to keep a healthy profit margin throughout the expansion. If you're unable to allocate funds to the EXPANSION account ahead of time, you still need to figure out how to carve out an allocation for your debt payment later. If your practice isn't profitable enough to do that ahead of growth, how can you be certain that it will be possible after growth? You can't, and that's how some practice owners get into trouble with debt.

If you want to take out a loan for growth, have a plan for exactly what you will do with the money. Map out how long it will take to pay off the loan. This should be a bank loan, not a predatory, high-fee loan. I don't want you to end up in a situation where you can't make payroll and are searching through your email for every loan offer you've ever received, trying to get some fast cash at the eleventh hour.

Another important consideration when using debt to fund growth is that small business loans often require the owner to personally guarantee the loan. That means that if the business defaults on the loan, the owner is personally responsible for paying it back. Even though the business is borrowing the money, you are still on the hook.

PHASE 3: YOUR NEW NORMAL

AT SOME POINT IN THE expansion process, your role within your practice may need to change. Specifically, you'll probably reduce your caseload to make more space for the work only *you* can do in the business. Increasingly, your role will shift from business operator to business owner. It is likely that there will come a point when you must do less work in the business as a clinician or burn out.

You can and should work in the area of the business that you love the most. For some practice owners, that will be stepping fully into the visionary role. For others, it might be taking on the clinical director role or supervising trainees. In my experience, practice owners keep doing noncritical things that they shouldn't be doing for way too long.

A business owner's role isn't necessarily to know how to do all the things, it's to find the right people to do the things. If you DIY the launch of your practice, you might resort to the "How can I figure this out?" or "How can I fix this?" bootstrap mindset as it grows. When faced with a problem, your first reaction might be to do the work yourself. As your practice grows, you will eventually experience a shift. It is beautifully described in the book *Who Not How* by Dan Sullivan and Dr. Benjamin Hardy. The authors suggest that, rather than ask yourself, "How do I solve this problem?" you ask, "Who (on my team) can solve the problem?[10]" Instead of being the fixer, you'll be the director of traffic, and it's a liberating transition. I encourage you to make this shift sooner than later. As your business grows, you as the owner can become increasingly laser-focused on *your* biggest contribution to the business and hire others to do what uses their own strengths.

As my team has grown over the years, the transition from individual contributor to manager to leader has been challenging for me at times. It's something I have had to actively work on each day. There have also been moments when my team had a difficult time adjusting, like when someone went from working with me directly to being part of a new chain of command. For me, the transition to leadership didn't just "happen." And if I'm facing an issue that I haven't figured out how to tackle yet, I tend to slip back into the individual contributor work, where it's easier to feel like I'm getting things accomplished. I recognize this pattern now and allow myself a little *doing* before going back to the work that only I can do.

> WHAT IS THE VALUE THAT ONLY YOU CAN BRING TO THE BUSINESS? AS YOUR PRACTICE GROWS, THAT SHOULD BE YOUR FOCUS.

Letting go of the mindset that you must do and know everything can be difficult. Yet it's an important milestone in a larger group practice. In fact, my clients who do less of the day-to-day work in their businesses and have clarity on their roles tend to be *more* profitable than the practices where the owner is still involved in everything. I believe it's related to having an abundance mindset, in which you believe you can afford to hire people and there will always be more clients—versus a scarcity mindset, in which you think there simply cannot be enough work or money for another team member. Of course, every business owner has moments when they wonder if the house of cards will come crashing down, but practice owners with an abundance mindset typically do better overall.

Kasey Compton is intentional about giving her team a decision framework when she removes herself from another portion of the daily operations. The framework keeps her team accountable for the department's metrics. Because she uses the Profit First accounts, Kasey also gives bank access to a few key team members. They can see only the bank accounts they are responsible for, like OpEx, not the full financial picture of the business. Because team members can see the OpEx account balance, they can make spending decisions on their own, further decreasing their reliance on Kasey.

If you've run the numbers and have a profitable model, scaling does mean you'll probably make more money after the growth phase. Enjoy the reward for your hard work!

TOO MUCH TOO SOON

Is it possible to grow too much too soon? Unfortunately, yes. It's so easy to get swept up in the excitement of a shiny new office. Visiting a beautiful building can be so much fun, and picking out furniture and décor can be a welcome distraction from the day-to-day monotony of the business.

Dawn Leprich-Graves, LCPC, PMH-C, owner of Bricolage Wellness in Illinois, was so excited to open her third location. She saw a space that seemed perfect. It was in a newly-constructed building, and she felt like she was getting a great rate for the lease because she was signing so early in the building process. She put down a deposit of $13,000 and signed a lease that included a $25,000 buildout allowance paid by the landlord and a $75,000 buildout allowance that would be wrapped into her lease. After the lease was signed, Dawn paid $12,000 to the builder as a deposit and asked for a buildout quote based on the needs of her practice. Dawn had budgeted to spend an additional $10,000, figuring that $110,000 should be enough for what she wanted. The builder's quote came back over $300,000. Dawn would have to come up with close to $200,000 in a few short months to complete the buildout. She tried to modify the plans to cut costs, but lower-end finishes didn't move the needle significantly. The amount of money she needed to come up with was so far out of reach that, after trying several iterations of plans, Dawn had to hire an attorney and get out of the lease. While that was the right thing to do, it was still an expensive mistake that cost Dawn her two deposits totaling $25,000 and about $10,000 in attorney fees.

This setback didn't deter Dawn, though. She was determined to find an office for her third location. A few months later, she found a new space that needed minimal improvement and fit her budget. She rented it for one year while she built up her reserves.

Then she bought a building and moved her third location to this beautiful new space. By slowing down just a little to lay out a plan, Dawn found herself in an even better situation that didn't put her practice and her family at risk.

I want to bring your attention to the fact that the "Planning" section of this chapter is much longer than the "Action" section. This is intentional. The planning of an expansion project should take some time. Expanding your business includes a degree of risk, and being intentional in the planning phase ensures that the growth won't leave you stretched so thin that the slightest issue puts your business in peril.

The biggest challenge with growing quickly is how vulnerable it can leave your practice if something goes wrong and you don't have enough money to carry you through. If your biller quits or insurance payments slow down, you're left in the lurch. If your office floods, you might not have the funds to pay for repairs before your insurance steps in. Emergencies happen, and being strapped for cash can be very stressful. The bigger the business, the more things can go wrong. It's not because you've failed; it's just how life goes.

In times of expansion and recession, the businesses that run out of cash are the ones that are less likely to make it. This can be an easy lesson to forget when times are good, but ultimately, cash is king when it comes to keeping a business afloat.

WHAT TO DO AFTER A TOO-FAST EXPANSION

IF IT FEELS LIKE THINGS are careening out of control, just remember that most problems are solvable. It's not guaranteed to be easy, but there is likely a solution. If you're in a tough financial position after growing too much too soon, try to be brutally honest with yourself. Look at your financials and meet with your accountant, or enlist your accountability partner to help you look at the situation objectively and figure out what's happening.

It's interesting to me that therapists can sometimes develop "ostrich syndrome" about their practice financials. They hide their heads in the sand, thinking that if they don't look, there is no danger ahead. Some therapists do this by avoiding their financial situation completely: They'll have a stack of unopened IRS letters and bank statements on their desk. They won't log in to their bank accounts and look at their account balances. They'll wince every time they run their credit card because they're unsure whether the transaction will clear. I've been the accountant reviewing the IRS letters and taking stock of the business when things aren't going well, and I've noticed two things: one, reality is not usually as bad as my client thinks it is; and two, every client breathes a huge sigh of relief when they finally *know* where they stand.

After you've assessed the situation, no solution should be off limits. Thinking about the situation creatively will lead you to the answer.

If the issue is cash flow, consider pausing growth for a few months so you can build back cash reserves. A line of credit or loan can help as a temporary stopgap, but it shouldn't be a permanent solution.

If you have more than one location, take a close look at how each location is doing financially. Is there a location that is always trailing behind, where it's hard to recruit clinicians or get new clients? Esther Boykin, LMFT, owner of Group Therapy Associates, was in this situation with one of her Northern Virginia offices. When we looked at the numbers, it was clear that one of her suburban locations was subsidizing the high rent in another city. The city office was in a competitive location, and the referrals just weren't enough for that office to break even. Esther felt like she was always on the brink of running out of money, so with this information, she made the difficult decision to close her city office. Her team continued to see their city clients through telehealth, and even though she did lose a few clinicians, the impact was minimal. The unintended benefit from Esther not being stretched so thin anymore was that she was able to focus on growing the suburban location when she was no longer focusing all her time and energy on trying to make the city location successful.

Now, I'm not saying that closing an office is always the solution. But if a location is draining your resources, closing it should be a consideration. Other options could be to sublet an office (or a few), renegotiate your lease if it is close to completion, or see if you can reduce the size of your office space.

If you have over-hired admin, can you temporarily reduce their hours? Can you talk to your team about how to do more with less? Can they increase call-to-client conversions to quickly bring in more income? These are all examples of creative problem-solving to boost income and decrease expenses.

QUIZ: ARE YOU READY TO EXPAND?

IF YOU HAVE EXPANSION IN mind, take this quiz to see if you are ready. You can also find the quiz at www.profitfirstfortherapists. com/tools, and the online version will calculate your score for you.

	Yes (2 points)	Sometimes (1 point)	No (0 points)
Does your bank account always have ample funds?			
Have you maximized the use of your existing space? For most practices, this will be at least six appointments per room per day.			
Have you maximized your existing team? For most practices, this means your clinicians see 80-90% or more of expected sessions (for example, 90% of twenty-five sessions per week, if that is the expectation).			
Have you always had enough funds for payroll for the last six months?			
Have you calculated the cost of the planned expansion?			
Do you have funds saved, or a plan for how you will pay for the cost of the expansion?			
Do you have at least one month's worth of expenses saved for emergencies?			
Have you calculated your estimated tax liability for the current year, and do you have the funds saved?			
Totals			
Total Points			

0–7 points: Expansion is in your future, but it's not time yet—hold off or you might put your practice at risk. Keep your focus on stabilizing the business finances until you have a reserve in each Profit First bank account and are able to cover the practice's monthly expenses with ease.

8–11 points: You are on the right track, but proceed with caution. There are some warning signs that your cash reserves are not quite strong enough for an expansion. Spend some time in the planning phase to lay out your plan. Start by allocating at least 1% to an EXPANSION bank account (more, if possible) until you have enough saved to fund an expansion.

12–16 points: You're ready! You have positioned your practice well for expansion. Make a plan and go for it.

DOS AND DON'TS FOR EXPANSION AND SCALING

IF YOU'RE PLANNING TO EXPAND your practice, here are a few simple dos and don'ts to help you along the way:

- Do make a budget.
- Do get quotes for a buildout before you make a commitment to a space.
- Do have a cash reserve in your EXPANSION account.
- Don't get too excited about something shiny and new.
- Don't assume everything will go perfectly because it won't.

Sometimes, when things aren't going well, it's easier to put your head down and *work* rather than truly examine what's going on under the hood of your business. That can look like taking on more clinical hours or inserting yourself where you haven't been needed. I get it; being a business owner is not for the faint of heart. Carefully planning your growth and expansion will set you up for success and pay dividends for years to come.

CLOSING

REMEMBER STACY, MY CLIENT WHO didn't have enough money for payroll? She first learned about Profit First at a conference, where she sat in the audience and heard Mike Michalowicz speak. Earlier that day, she had chatted about her business with colleagues and told them it was doing great. She had twelve clinicians and two locations, and she carried on as if life was good.

She told me, "As I heard Mike speak, surrounded by people I knew, I felt like the biggest fraud ever. While I'd been pretending everything was fine, at that very moment, I had negative four thousand dollars in my bank account. Negative. Below zero. I knew that I'd probably be getting another bounced payment notification by the end of the day."

Stacy put on a brave face, but she was broke. She had been busting her tail day in and day out for more than ten years and had nothing to show for it. She had a pile of unopened IRS letters on her desk taunting her about the back taxes she owed, and her crappy marriage was draining every ounce of energy she had left.

That fateful day when she heard Mike speak, Stacy decided that she couldn't give up. She hadn't come this far to stop and quit, and she decided to give Profit First a try.

A few weeks later, she gave me a call. I could tell that she was truly ready to make a change. When we started implementing Profit First, we quickly realized that Stacy's clinician compensation was too high. It was painful for her to sit across from her team and renegotiate their contracts.

"I thought I was going to die of shame," she told me. But she kept going.

Fast forward six months, and payroll hadn't bounced once, there was enough in the TAX account to make her quarterly estimated tax payment, and Stacy wasn't waking up in a cold sweat in the middle of the night worrying about money.

There were lots of little tweaks and adjustments to make along the way; there still are every time a new location is added, or another significant change happens in the practice. But for the first time since starting her business, Stacy (and her now ex-husband) no longer owe any back taxes. Last year was the first year she fully funded her 401(k). She is paying cash for her daughter's college education and has enough money to replace her nine-year-old car and take a trip when she wants to.

Stacy's practice is finally serving *her*.

At the same time, it's serving her team. At a recent meeting, she shared a text message she'd just received from a team member: "I don't want to sound corny, but I just want you to know that I love working here and I love the people I work with! Thank you for trusting me and hiring me."

As tears filled Stacy's eyes, I could see how proud she is of what she's accomplished.

I can't help but imagine how different her life would be today had she not decided to take the leap. Then I think of all the clients of my firm, whose businesses and lives are changed forever thanks to Profit First. And I can't help but think that if my mother had had the opportunity to use Profit First for the sewing shop, the phone book, or any of the businesses in between, she would have had a fighting chance at making a living doing what she loved. It's not too late for you. I truly know that Profit First can change the trajectory of your life if you'll let it. I hope you do.

EPILOGUE

In my memories, writing this book will always be intertwined with my mother's illness. I started writing shortly before my sister and I became her caregivers. ALS is a dreadful disease with no cure, and I watched, helpless, as my mother progressively lost the ability to eat, speak, walk, and stand. As it happened, I pushed hard, writing every day, knowing I'd need to take a break as the end neared.

While the disease progressed, Mom and I had many slow conversations about life through Suzette, the robotic voice of her tablet's speech app. Despite her efforts, my mother never had a successful business. She had no regrets, though; in the end, all that mattered was the time we had together. She was incredibly proud of her two daughters and five grandchildren. That was enough.

During the last few days in the hospital, it became increasingly difficult to communicate. Mom could only move one finger by that point, so typing took a long time. I didn't mind. I had nowhere else to be, and I knew time was running out. My sister and I dug deep into our bank of happy childhood memories, telling story after story and helping Mom remember all the good times we had together. She communicated mostly in smiles and nods, the emotion of each story visible in her ice-blue eyes. We sat with her as she took her last breath. After a long goodbye, my mother passed away peacefully on January 14, 2022.

Nothing about losing a parent is easy. In those last few weeks, I was physically and mentally present through the beauty and the pain. I wasn't distracted by my business because I knew it would be there when I got back, and that it would continue to provide for my family and my team while I showed up fully for something that mattered so much. That was a gift I couldn't have expected when I started my Profit First journey years ago, and I will always be grateful for it.

APPENDIX 1

Tax Basics for Private Practice

Tax compliance isn't exactly exciting for most therapists, so I'm including some tax basics for you to use as a reference guide. The United States tax code is tens of thousands of pages long, so please note that not all scenarios are covered here, and that these items likely do not apply if you do not live or work in the United States.

Tax entities and tax forms:

1040 – You will use this form to file your personal tax return. The tax return is due on April 15 or the next business day. You may also file an extension, which will extend the tax filing deadline to October 15 or the next business day.

Schedule C – You will file this tax form with your 1040 (personal tax return) if you run your business as a sole proprietor or have a single-member limited liability company or professional limited liability company (LLC or PLLC).

1120S – You will file this tax return if your business is an S corporation, a professional corporation (PC) taxed as an

S corporation, or an LLC taxed as an S corporation. For a fiscal year ending on December 31, this tax return is due on March 15 or the next business day, and K-1s (see the following) must be issued to each shareholder by March 15 as well. You may file an extension, which will extend the tax filing deadline to September 15 or the next business day.

1065 – You will file this tax return if your business is a partnership or multimember LLC. For a fiscal year ending on December 31, this tax return is due on March 15 or the next business day, and K-1s (see the following) must be issued to each shareholder by March 15 as well. You may file an extension, which will extend the tax filing deadline to September 15 or the next business day.

1120 – You will file this tax return if your business is a C corporation (note: this is rare in private practice). For a fiscal year ending on December 31, this tax return is due on April 15 or the next business day. You may also file an extension, which will extend the tax filing deadline to October 15 or the next business day.

990 – You will file this tax return if the business you manage is a nonprofit (note: this is rare in private practice). For a fiscal year ending on December 31, this tax return is due on May 15 or the next business day. You may also file an extension, which will extend the tax filing deadline to November 15 or the next business day.

K-1 – This form is issued to a shareholder or partner and reports each shareholder/partner's share of income, losses, deductions, and credits. The shareholder uses this information to report the income, losses, deductions, and credits on their personal tax return (1040).

Flow-through entities (also known as pass-through entities): Businesses that file a Schedule C, 1120S, or 1065 are flow-through entities that do not pay taxes at the federal level. The profit of the business "flows through" to the personal tax return of the owner, partner, or shareholder, where it is taxed on Form 1040. The entity may be required to pay state tax (this varies by state).

Quarterly estimated tax: If you expect to owe more than $1,000 in tax when your personal tax return (1040) is filed, you are required to pay quarterly estimated taxes. You must pay at least 100% of last year's total tax (110% if your adjusted gross income, or AGI, is over $150,000 or over $75,000 for those married filing separately), or 90% of this year's total tax to avoid penalties and interest. Estimated tax payments are due on:

Q1: April 15
Q2: June 15
Q3: September 15
Q4: January 15 of the following year

To calculate quarterly estimated tax payments, you can use IRS form 1040-ES or ask your tax preparer to calculate the amount due.

One common misconception about quarterly estimated tax payments is that if you make the payments generated with your prior year's tax return in full, you won't have a balance due. If your income remains similar to the previous year, that may be the case; but if your income increases, you'll likely owe more. Let's look at an example to see how that might work:

Year 1: Your taxable income is $100,000. Based on your previous year's total tax, you make estimated payments of $4,000/quarter for Year 2.

Year 2: When the year is over, your taxable income is $120,000. Your total tax is $20,000, and you have made four quarterly payments of $4,000 $20,000 $16,000 = $4,000 balance due. You will not owe penalties or interest for underpayment because you paid 100% of the previous year's tax, but you must pay the remaining balance due with your tax return.

Self-employment tax: Self-employment tax, also known as FICA, includes Social Security and Medicare. If you've ever been an employee, you may have noticed a Social Security and Medicare withholding on your W-2 or paystub. Employees have 7.65% of their wages withheld for Social Security and Medicare, and employers contribute an additional 7.65% of wages (up to a wage cap that increases annually). When you are self-employed, you have the privilege of paying both the employee and the employer portions of Social Security and Medicare, for a total of 15.3%. This is calculated on your personal tax return (1040) and paid with your tax due or quarterly estimated tax payments. Because both the employee and employer portions of self-employment tax are paid by the individual, however, there is a deduction for half the amount of the self-employment tax.

Extensions: An extension to file your tax return is not an extension to pay. All taxes are considered due on the due date of your tax return, not the extended due date. If you expect to owe a payment with your tax return and do not make a payment when you file an extension, you will owe penalties and interest on the balance due.

What is tax-deductible: To deduct an expense, it must be ordinary and necessary. That means that the amount is reasonable and the expense is commonly accepted in the industry. Note that the expense does not need to be indispensable to the business. For example, you can certainly run a practice without paying for ads; however, advertising is commonly accepted as a deduction in the mental health industry.

What is not tax-deductible: Personal expenses. Business meals are only 50% deductible (although restaurant meals were temporarily 100% deductible in 2021 and 2022). Owner's draws or distributions are not deductible business expenses. Penalties are typically nondeductible. The principal portion of a loan payment is nondeductible.

Deducting things that aren't deductible because there is no oversight: If you DIY your bookkeeping and taxes, there is a good chance that you've deducted an expense that isn't tax-deductible at some point. If your tax return is selected for audit, should a deduction be incorrect or unsupported, it will be removed and you will owe additional tax, penalties, and interest. An accuracy-related penalty could also be assessed. I highly recommend that you work with a professional tax preparer as a business owner.

Receipt management: The taxpayer is responsible for keeping complete and accurate records to document their expenses. You can use software, a cloud folder, or a simple envelope to store all business receipts. Be particularly mindful of transactions that could *look* personal, like big box or grocery store purchases. When it comes to business meals, you'll want to note the attendees and business purpose of the meal on the receipt as well. You won't need these receipts unless your tax return is selected for audit, but if it is, you'll be happy you took the time to keep your records.

Progressive tax brackets: Have you ever heard someone say, "I'd rather not make more money because I'll owe more in taxes?" This is a common misconception, and the good news is that it is incorrect. In the United States, we have progressive tax brackets. As you move up to the next tax bracket, the next dollar earned is taxed at the new rate, not your entire income.

For example, a single taxpayer with $100,000 of taxable income (after deductions) will pay $17,400 in tax for 2023.

They will pay 10% on the first $11,000 of taxable income, 12% on the taxable income between $11,000 and $44,725, 22% on the taxable income between $44,725 and $95,375, and finally, 24% on the taxable income between $95,375 and $100,000. Their next taxable dollar would be taxed at 24%.

2023 Federal Income Tax Brackets and Rates for Single Filers, Married Couples Filing Jointly, and Heads of Households			
Tax Rate	**For Single Filers**	**For Married Individuals Filing Joint Returns**	**For Heads of Households**
10%	$0–$11,000	$0–$22,000	$0–$15,700
12%	$11,000 –$44,725	$22,000–$89,450	$15,700–$59,850
22%	$44,725–$95,375	$89,450–$190,750	$59,850–$95,350
24%	$95,375–$182,100	$190,750–$364,200	$95,350–$182,100
32%	$182,100–$231,250	$364,200–$462,500	$182,100–$231,250
35%	$231,250–$578,125	$462,500–$693,750	$231,250–$578,100
37%	$578,125 or more	$693,750 or more	$578,100 or more

Table A.1: 2023 Federal Income Tax Brackets

Note: Tax brackets change each year; a simple online search will show up-to-date tax brackets.

S corporations: S corporations *can* make sense for some business owners. However, I often see incorrect advice being shared in industry membership groups. If you are considering making an S election for your LLC, PLLC, or PC, I highly recommend speaking to an accountant to make sure that this will have a positive tax impact for you. There are additional compliance costs attached to an S corporation, such as a payroll system and an additional tax return, so you'll want to make sure the potential tax benefits outweigh the additional expense.

Additionally, some states tax S corporations as C corporations, which can create a huge surprise tax bill and offset the tax savings at the federal level.

Reasonable compensation: S corporations are required to pay the owner a "reasonable wage" through payroll. The goal here is to keep the wage or salary as low as is reasonable to maximize tax savings. You are not required to take a salary so large that it will put the business at a loss. If you aren't on payroll yet, you should not take an owner's distribution or pay any personal expenses through the business. What happens if you don't pay yourself a reasonable salary? Under audit, a portion (or all) or your distributions can be recharacterized as wages. You'll owe FICA (Social Security and Medicare) as well as penalties and interest for the late payments.

Cash vs. accrual: Your business accounting records and tax return will be on either a cash or accrual basis. Most private practices are cash basis taxpayers because it is a simpler (and less expensive) way to record business activity. The accrual method isn't required by the IRS until a business has average gross receipts of $25 million for the last three years. The accounting method you use will be noted on your tax return.

Cash basis: Income is recognized when it is received, and expenses are recognized when they are paid. You won't see accounts receivable or accounts payable on cash basis books.

Accrual basis: Income is recognized when it is earned, and expenses are recognized when they are accrued.

> Example 1: You see a client in December, submit an insurance claim, and receive payment in January. Cash basis books will recognize the income in January, when it was received. Accrual basis books will recognize the income in December, when it was earned.

> Example 2: You pay a cleaning service on the first day of each month, when they send you an invoice for the previous month's work. On January 1, you receive an invoice for the cleaning done in December and pay it on January 5. Cash basis books will recognize the expense in January, when the invoice was paid. Accrual basis books will recognize the expense in December, when the work was done.

> It's easy to see how accrual can complicate things significantly.

APPENDIX 2

Making Sense of Your Financial Reports

IF YOU DON'T HAVE AN accounting degree, reading your financial reports can be overwhelming. Let's go over the basics of the reports you'll review most often as a business owner and what information they present. The three most common reports are the P&L, the balance sheet, and the statement of cash flow. QuickBooks Online is my preferred accounting software, so I'll use its terminology here; just know that if you use a different software, the report will show the same information but the wording might be slightly different.

PROFIT AND LOSS (ALSO CALLED THE INCOME STATEMENT OR P&L)

THE P&L IS THE ACCOUNTING equation: Income – Expenses = Net Income (also known as profit). Below the report name you will see the reporting period, and at the very bottom you will see if the report is cash or accrual.

Profit and Loss

January – February, 2023

		Total
Income		
Therapy Income		103,380.00
Total Income	$	**103,380.00**
GROSS PROFIT	$	**103,380.00**
Expenses		
Overhead Expenses		
Advertising and Marketing		2,306.00
Continuing Education		1,090.00
Credit Card Processing		1,033.80
Legal and Professional Services		1,270.00
Office Software		826.00
Office Supplies		1,872.00
Telephone		728.00
Total Overhead Expenses	$	**9,125.80**
Payroll Expenses		
Administrative Compensation		
Administrative Wages		7,480.00
Administrative Payroll Tax		598.40
Total Administrative Compensation	$	**8,078.40**
Officer Compensation		
Officer Wages		8,000.00
Officer Payroll Tax		640.00
Total Officer Compensation		8,640.00
Other Payroll Expenses		
Health Insurance Contribution		790.00
Total Other Payroll Expenses	$	**790.00**
Therapist Compensation		
Therapist Wages		55,927.00
Therapist Payroll Tax		4,762.00
Total Therapist Wages	$	**60,689.00**
Total Payroll Expenses	$	**78,197.40**
Rent and Lease		2,700.00
Total Expenses	$	**90,023.20**
NET OPERATING INCOME	$	**13,356.80**
NET INCOME	$	**13,356.80**

Cash Basis

INCOME REPRESENTS THE GROSS RECEIPTS in your business, minus any refunds.

Cost of Goods Sold (COGS): Some practice owners like to see their clinical labor costs in this section; personally, I like to see it under the Expenses section. Because it won't affect the deductibility of your labor, either works. You won't see this line item if you don't have an amount in that expense category.

GROSS PROFIT: Income – COGS = Gross Profit. This is the preliminary profit after COGS.

Expenses: You'll see a listing of all your expense categories in this section.

NET OPERATING INCOME: Gross Profit – Expenses = Net Operating Income. Sometimes this will match your Net Income and sometimes it won't, depending on what is found in Other Income and Other Expenses.

Other Income: This is where you'll find income that is separately stated on your tax return or out of the ordinary. Some examples might include interest income, credit card rewards, federal or state credits, etc. (There is no Other Income on the sample P&L.)

Other Expenses: In this section, you'll see items like amortization and depreciation, penalties, and nondeductible expenses. (There is no Other Expenses on the sample P&L.)

NET INCOME: Net Operating Income + Other Income – Expenses – Other Expenses = Net Income. This is your final profit after all adjustments have been made. This amount may not match the net income on your tax return because of nondeductible items, and that's normal.

BALANCE SHEET

THE BALANCE SHEET SHOWS A different accounting equation: Assets = Liabilities + Equity. If you're using an accounting software, these will always balance. If you're using a spreadsheet… maybe not. The balance sheet is always a snapshot in time. Let's say you run the report on December 31. It will be a snapshot of that specific day and will most certainly change the next day.

Balance Sheet

As of January 31, 2023

	Total
ASSETS	
Current Assets	
Bank Accounts	
Checking 1234	79,873.75
Savings 4321	18,354.00
Total Bank Accounts	$ **98,227.75**
Other Current Assets	
Undeposited Funds	0.00
Total Other Current Assets	$ **0.00**
Total Current Assets	$ **98,227.75**
Fixed Assets	
Security Deposit	2,700.00
Leasehold Improvement	6,500.00
Total Fixed Assets	$ **9,200.00**
TOTAL ASSETS	$ **107,427.75**
LIABILITIES AND EQUITY	
Liabilities	
Current Liabilities	
Credit Cards	
Credit Card 0000	3,954.39
Total Credit Cards	$ **3,954.39**
Total Current Liabilities	$ **3,954.39**
Long-Term Liabilities	
Bank Loan	8,745.00
Total Long-Term Liabilities	$ **8,745.00**
Total Liabilities	$ **12,699.39**
Equity	
Additional Paid in Capital	20,000.00
Owner's Distribution	−30,750.00
Retained Earnings	92,121.56
Net Income	13,356.80
Total Equity	$ **94,728.36**
TOTAL LIABILITIES AND EQUITY	$ **107,427.75**

ASSETS: This section includes the bank balances of all Bank Accounts on the last day included in the report (in this example, January 31), Security Deposits, Fixed Assets > $2,500, and the remaining amount due on any Loans issued by the company to others (like the owner, for example). On accrual reports, this will also include Accounts Receivable. Most private practices are cash basis, so they will not see Accounts Receivable on this report. This information will remain in your EHR software to avoid duplication, but also to maintain HIPAA compliance.

Liabilities: This section includes the amount owed on any liabilities on the last day of the report (in this example, January 31). This may include Credit Cards, Loans, and payroll liabilities like Payroll Tax or Benefits Payable. On accrual reports, this section will also include Accounts Payable.

Equity: Equity is the owner's (or owners') remaining equity in the business. This section includes Paid-in Capital (your initial contribution to the business), additional Owner's Contributions, Owner's Draws or Distributions, and Net Income. The profit of the business lives in this section because it is ultimately part of the owner's equity. At the end of each year, Net Income becomes Retained Earnings, and any Contributions and Distributions from the previous year are netted against this number. Let's look at an example:

Here is the Equity section on December 31:

Owner's Contribution: $10,000

Owner's Distribution: –$90,000

Retained Earnings: $0 (this is rare, but for the simplicity of this example I'm using $0)

Net Income: $140,000

Total Equity: $10,000 – $90,000 + $140,000 = $60,000

Here is the same Equity section on January 1:

Owner's Contribution: $0

Owner's Distribution: $0

Retained Earnings: $60,000

Net Income: $0

Total Equity: $60,000

STATEMENT OF CASH FLOWS

THIS REPORT SHOWS THE CASH flow of the business because it can often be different from the P&L. If you ever find yourself wondering, *Where did all the profit go?* this is the report for you. On this report, a negative number shows money flowing *out* of the business, whereas a positive number shows money flowing *into* the business. This report shows what your profit was used for, like paying down loans, paying taxes, and paying yourself.

Statement of Cash flows
January 31, 2023

	Total
OPERATING ACTIVITIES	
Net Income	13,356.80
Adjustments to Reconcile Net Income to Net Cash Provided by Operations:	
Chase Credit card 0000	– 1,587.00
Total Adjustments to Reconcile Net Income to Net Cash Provided by Operations:	– $ 1,587.00
Net Cash Provided by Operating Activities	$ 11,769.80
FINANCING ACTIVITIES	
Bank Loan	–799.00
Owner's Distribution	–2,000.00
Net Cash Provided by Financing Activities	–$ 2,799.00
Net Cash Increase for Period	$ 8,970.80
Cash at Beginning of Period	89,256.95
Cash at End of Period	$ 98,227.75

OPERATING ACTIVITIES: This section calculates the amount of cash added to the business based on the Net Income and any Adjustments.

Net Income: This section shows the Net Income for the period of your report.

Adjustments to reconcile Net Income to Net Cash: This is the meat of the report. It shows where your money is going. Credit card and benefit payments show up here. You expensed the transactions on your credit card before making the credit card payment, so this section shows the funds being used to pay the credit card down, even though you have already recorded all the expenses. (You can only deduct the expenses paid by credit card, not the credit card payment.)

INVESTING ACTIVITIES: For most practices, this section shows Security Deposits, Leasehold Improvements, or other investments made. (Please note that in the previous example, there are no investing activities, which is why the section does not appear.)

FINANCING ACTIVITIES: Loan payments appear in this section. If you received a new loan from a bank, you'll see a positive number; if you paid down a loan, you'll see a negative number. You'll also see Distributions and Owner's draws in this section.

Cash at Beginning of Period: This is the cash balance on the first date of the report. If your report is for January 1 – March 31, this section will show the cash balance on January 1.

Cash at End of Period: Cash at Beginning of Period + Operating Activities + Adjustments + Financing Activities = Cash at End of Period.

APPENDIX 3

The Key Financial Systems in Your Practice

THERE ARE FIVE MAIN FINANCIAL systems in your practice:

- Billing
- Payroll
- Accounting/Bookkeeping
- Tax
- Profit First

Whether your systems are intentional or not, they are there. A thoughtfully designed system tends to be more efficient than a "This is how we've always done it and all the information is in my brain" system and, over time, all systems will evolve—especially if your practice is growing.

BILLING: THE SYSTEM THAT KEEPS CASH COMING IN

I WHOLEHEARTEDLY BELIEVE THAT YOU should be paid well for the important work you do. When you bill your clients (or their insurance) for their sessions, you are doing them a favor.

You are making sure that you will stay in business and that your business will be there to continue working with them. Remember, your clients want your practice to be profitable so that you can be fully present with them in the therapy room.

I say this because billing must be a priority. Money simply must keep coming into the business on a regular business for it to succeed. Setting up strong systems to ensure that is your responsibility as a business owner, employer, and clinician. Automate as much as possible and create redundancy whenever possible so that the entire system does not rely on a single person. If you have a team, you know that it can be dangerous for only one person to know how to submit insurance billing. If they get sick or suddenly quit, you find yourself in a mess. I'm not saying that *you* should be the backup. I'm saying that *someone* should be a backup to keep things moving along. The larger the team, the more critical redundancy will be.

Another request I have is to make it easy for your clients to pay you. No practice owner likes paying credit card processing fees, but keeping your clients' credit card information on file for automatic payment processing reduces the barrier to collecting payment and often makes your services more accessible.

Years ago, Tamara had a private-pay practice that only accepted check or cash payments. When I asked how things were going, she'd say that she was having a hard time keeping her clinicians' schedules full. When we talked about the option of accepting credit card payments, she'd tell me, "I don't want to pay the credit card fees!"

I get it, no one likes paying the 2%–3% fees, even though they are tax-deductible. But the harder you make it for clients to pay you (because who carries a checkbook anymore?), the harder it will be to attract and keep your ideal clients. Tamara was losing thousands of dollars each month to save less than $100. Make it easy for clients to pay you. Most EHRs have payment processing capabilities and will automatically record the payments.

Similarly, another client of my firm would only accept payment through a third-party credit card processor because it was slightly cheaper than processing payments directly through her EHR (again, the fees). Because of HIPAA, payment processors that are outside of your EHR typically can't sync or communicate with it. That meant that each payment had to be manually recorded in the EHR, or the accounts receivable report would be incorrect and useless. That has a domino effect. It's easy to make a mistake, duplicate a payment, or omit one altogether. But most importantly, it takes a significant amount of time to record and reconcile the payments, and that is not an efficient use of your or your team's time. When we ran the numbers, it turned out that the hours my client was paying her admin to reconcile the payments amounted to almost double what the credit card fees would cost. Let's stop the madness! It's not worth saving a few pennies.

Another consideration before building your billing system is where you want your business to be in five years. It should be scalable, whether it's just you or you have fifty employees. Think of Tamara's front office. If she had continued to accept only checks or cash and had fifty clinicians, each seeing twenty-five clients per week, that would be 1,250 checks each week (or 250 each business day). No thank you.

I often hear solo practice owners say that they don't like billing, so they avoid it for weeks at a time. That makes their cash flow lumpy and their money tight in those weeks when there isn't much, or any, money coming into the practice. I want you to value getting paid. A grocery store doesn't feel guilty about charging you for a loaf of bread. If you aren't going to spend the needed time on your billing system to make things run smoothly in your practice, it's perfectly fine for you to say, "This is something that is important to my practice, but I don't want to be the person doing this. I am willing to spend some money on a biller so I don't have to do this task."

I want to mention that although billing deals with money, it is the one financial system that your accountant typically won't be a part of. An accountant may review your revenue reports, as my team does, but they usually won't submit insurance claims, record payments, manage your EHR, or audit your electronic remittance advice (ERA).

ACCOUNTING AND BOOKKEEPING: THE SYSTEM THAT HELPS YOU MAKE DECISIONS

YOUR BOOKKEEPING SYSTEM MIGHT BE a spreadsheet or software (I vote for software), but it should be *something*. There is so much precious data in the financial reports—don't let it go to waste by ignoring it until year-end. Tracking your income and expenses regularly will help you understand where your money is going and what is happening in your practice.

As you select your system, think about where you'd like your business to be in five years and what that will require. Your beautiful spreadsheet might work for you as a solo practice owner, but if you eventually need help from your accountant, bookkeeper, or admin because you plan to grow the practice, it probably won't work. If you already have an accountant, it's appropriate to ask them what system they use or prefer to help set yourself up to eventually outsource this task.

To protect yourself, I highly recommend that you keep your business and personal life separate. A separate bank account is always a must, even if you are a sole proprietor. If your business is a limited liability company (LLC), a professional limited liability company (PLLC), or a corporation (S corporation or C corporation), the bank account(s) should be in the business name, not yours. This helps protect your personal assets in the unlikely event that your business gets sued.

When you work with an accounting professional on a regular basis, they can leverage your financial data to help you look around the corner and anticipate opportunities or changes. When the perfect office space is available for rent, you'll have the data to know if you're ready to make the move or not. When your team asks for benefits, you'll know what you can afford. If your personal situation changes, for example, if your spouse gets laid off or a child gets sick and you suddenly need to take more money home, you'll know what you need to do to make it work.

If I were to ask any of my clients, "Do you make a concerted effort to keep your personal life out of the therapy room?" I am certain that all of them would answer, "Of course I do, because it's my ethical responsibility!" If you had the same thought, I'd like you to consider keeping your business and your personal finances separate an ethical responsibility.

Building a solid foundation in your accounting system is yet another way that you can be a good steward of the money in your practice. With financial reports to review, you can make decisions based on data instead of feelings to ensure the long-term success of your business.

PAYROLL: THE SYSTEM THAT PAYS YOUR TEAM

THE MOST IMPORTANT PART OF the payroll system is to build trust. Your employees need to know that they can count on their paycheck being accurate and on time. Anything less will quickly erode the trust they have in you and your practice. Jamara once told me the story of why she went into private practice. She had just started a new position at an agency, making more money than she'd ever made before. Her first paycheck was one day late. Because she was new, she thought at first that she may have mixed up the payroll days. As she asked around, she soon learned from her colleagues that this was a regular occurrence. Then the executive director mentioned that they were having cash flow issues and that payroll was always a little tight. Jamara decided then and there that she would eventually start her own private practice so she wouldn't have to rely on someone else to manage funds properly.

We are all humans, and mistakes will happen on occasion. A commission payment will be slightly off, deductions may be entered incorrectly—an error is bound to happen once in a while. You can recover from that by being fair, apologetic, transparent, and swift in correcting the issue. If payroll errors are common and consistent, your team will quickly come to resent you and retention will be challenging.

As far as making sure you have enough funds for payroll, Profit First will help smooth out the ups and downs, or make it obvious that there are issues to fix. When revenue is high, you'll transfer more than you need to your PAYROLL account. That extra cushion of money will stay there until a leaner period, and you can use the funds to make up the difference.

What about the rest of the payroll system? Do you sometimes overthink things? Payroll is an area that often gets overcomplicated for no good reason.

No matter the compensation structure you choose for your team, it should be simple, understandable, and scalable. Your team members should be able to clearly understand when they get paid and how, and they should also be clear on how they can make more money if they want to.

There is some significant overlap between the fields of accounting, law, and financial planning. Hiring employees or contractors and deciding how to pay them falls within both accounting and law. This is one of those areas where an ounce of prevention is worth a pound of cure. I explained compensation models extensively in Chapter 10, but it's always a good idea to check with an employment attorney in your state so you are aware of what is legally required of you. Mistakes can be expensive, so it's worth paying for a consultation to set yourself up for success. Several states make it difficult to hire contractors in your main field of business (therapy), others require an employer to pay for every minute worked, and a handful of states have very few restrictions at all.

You'll also want to protect yourself and your business by getting workers' compensation insurance and liability insurance and issuing 1099s and W-2s to your team at the end of the year.

TAX: THE SYSTEM THAT KEEPS YOU IN COMPLIANCE

AS A BUSINESS OWNER, YOU will owe tax on the profit generated in your business. Your tax liability will be calculated on your annual tax return, and depending on how much you owe, you may be required to make quarterly estimated tax payments throughout the year. (For more detail on taxes, see Appendix 1.)

Listen, I fully realize that no one gets excited about paying taxes. If you don't pay taxes, that means your business isn't profitable. Although zero taxes may sound tempting, I want more for your practice than zero profit.

I highly recommend that you work with a tax professional when you have a business. Taxation is much more complicated than when you're an employee receiving a W-2, and you don't know what you don't know. Also, there are lots of tax-planning strategies available to small business owners that will minimize your tax burden, so working with a professional can save you much more than it costs.

Mike contacted my team after receiving a few notices from the IRS that left him confused. "These notices say I didn't file my business tax returns for the last two years, and I know I filed them. What's going on?" When Mike shared a copy of the notices and the tax returns, the problem became painfully obvious: He hadn't filed the right form. His do-it-yourself taxes ended up costing him far more in penalties and interest than he would have paid to an accountant or tax preparer. He also hadn't realized that his partnership tax return was due on March 15 instead of the personal tax return deadline of April 15. Cue more penalties and interest.

The IRS waits for no one, and tax mistakes can be costly. Unless you're certain you know exactly what is expected of you, work with a tax professional.

PROFIT FIRST: THE SYSTEM THAT BRINGS IT ALL TOGETHER

PROFIT FIRST IS THE SYSTEM that bring all your other financial systems together to manage your practice. It connects the dots between billing, payroll, bookkeeping, and tax to give you clear metrics on how your practice is performing.

If you were ever to step out of your business (temporarily or permanently), this system would help your team make decisions, manage cash flow, and keep things moving along. It gives you and your team the data you need to keep the practice running like a well-oiled machine.

Over time, Profit First will prove to be a fundamental piece of your business, and you'll use it as a framework to make critical decisions.

APPENDIX 4

Target Allocations for Each Stage of Private Practice

Target Allocation Percentages (TAPs)				
	Solo	Small Group	Medium Group	Large Group
OpEx – Operating Expenses	10–40%	15–35%	10–25%	10–18%
Payroll – Therapists	0%	25–45%	45–60%	45–60%
Payroll – Admin	0–5%	0–5%	0–8%	4–7%
Payroll – Leadership	0%	0%	0%	3–5%
Payroll – Owner or Owner's Pay	30–60%	10–30%	5–10%	5–10%
Tax	5–35%	5–25%	5–15%	5–15%
Profit	5–15%	5–15%	5–10%	5–10%

APPENDIX 5

Instant Assessment

	Actual	CAP%	TAP%	PF$	The Bleed	The Fix
Real Revenue	A1					
OpEx – Operating Expenses	A2	B2	C2	D2	E2	F2
Payroll – Therapists	A3	B3	C3	D3	E3	F3
Payroll – Admin	A4	B4	C4	D4	E4	F4
Payroll – Leadership (if applicable)	A5	B5	C5	D5	E5	F5
Payroll – Owner (if applicable)	A6	B6	C6	D6	E6	F6
Owner's Pay (if applicable)	A7	B7	C7	D7	E7	F7
Tax	A8	B8	C8	D8	E8	F8
Profit	A9	B9	C9	D9	E9	F9
Totals	A10	B10	C10	D10	E10	F10

APPENDIX 6

Transfer Calculator

	CAPs	Transfers
INCOME Bank Balance		
OpEx – Operating Expenses		
Payroll – Therapists		
Payroll – Admin		
Payroll – Leadership (if applicable)		
Payroll – Owner (if applicable)		
Total Payroll		
Owner's Pay (if applicable)		
Tax		
Profit		
	100%	

APPENDIX 7

Getting Started Checklist and Process Summary

1. Open three business checking accounts using your current bank. Ask for checks and a debit card for each if needed.
   a. OpEx
   b. Payroll (if needed)
   c. Owner's Pay
2. Open two business savings accounts.
   a. Profit
   b. Tax
3. Your existing business checking account becomes your Income account.
4. Determine which target allocations (TAPs) you will use (Appendix 4).
5. Complete the Instant Assessment (Appendix 5).
6. Decide on transfer frequency (weekly, biweekly, twice monthly on the tenth and twenty-fifth, or monthly).
7. Make your initial transfers with the Transfer Calculator (Appendix 6).

Each transfer day (weekly, biweekly, on the tenth and twenty-fifth of each month, or monthly):

1. Transfer funds from your Income account to the PROFIT, TAX, PAYROLL, OWNER'S PAY, and OPEX accounts based on your CAPs. Combine all the *Payroll* line items into one transfer.
2. Look at the balance of each account to make sure there are enough funds for the expected expenses. If not, consider deferring an expense or do some troubleshooting to find out why there isn't enough money in the account.
3. Trust the process.

Quarterly:

1. Pay your quarterly estimated tax payment or the amount due with your tax return from your TAX account. (If there is any money left, leave it!)
2. Take half of the balance in your PROFIT account for yourself. Leave the other half in the account as an emergency fund.
3. Review the CAPs to TAPs worksheet and adjust your current allocations (CAPs) to the next quarterly step toward your target allocations (TAPs).
4. Trust the process.

You can find a downloadable copy of this Process Summary at www.profitfirstfortherapists.com/tools.

APPENDIX 8

Lifestyle Worksheet

	Current $	Nice to Have $
Mortgage or rent		
Car, insurance, and fuel		
Groceries		
Restaurants and meal delivery		
Utilities		
Clothing		
Gifts		
Activities (gym, kids' activities, etc.)		
Amazon (in my budget, Amazon has its own line item)		
Insurance (life, home, umbrella, etc.)		
Daycare/child care (if applicable)		
Services (cleaning, landscaping, etc.)		
Travel		
Fun money		
Retirement and investment		
Education and student loans		
Donations		
(Additional category that applies to you)		
(Additional category that applies to you)		
TOTAL:		

APPENDIX 9

Reverse-Engineer Your Practice Worksheet

1	Desired take-home pay (from your Lifestyle Worksheet)	
2	*Owner's Pay* CAP (from your Instant Assessment)	
3	Monthly average revenue (Desired take-home pay from row 1/ *Owner's Pay* CAP from row 2)	
4	Average fee per session	
5	Number of monthly sessions needed to meet revenue goal* (Monthly average revenue from row 3/Average fee per session from row 4)	

APPENDIX 10

Expansion Quiz

	Yes (2 points)	Sometimes (1 point)	No (0 points)
Does your bank account always have ample funds?			
Have you maximized the use of your existing space? For most practices, this will be at least six appointments per room per day.			
Have you maximized your existing team? For most practices, this means your clinicians see 80-90% or more of expected sessions (for example, 90% of twenty-five sessions per week, if that is the expectation).			
Have you always had enough funds for payroll for the last six months?			
Have you calculated the cost of the planned expansion?			
Do you have funds saved, or a plan for how you will pay for the cost of the expansion?			

	Yes (2 points)	Sometimes (1 point)	No (0 points)
Do you have at least one month's worth of expenses saved for emergencies?			
Have you calculated your estimated tax liability for the current year, and do you have the funds saved?			
Totals			
Total Points			

ENDNOTES

Foreword

[1] U.S. Bureau of Labor Statistics, "Marriage and family therapists." United States Department of Labor, https://data.bls.gov/search/query/results?q=Marriage%20and%20family%20therapists, last accessed November 30, 2022.

Chapter 1

[2] Mike Michalowicz, *Profit First* (Boonton, NJ: Obsidian Launch, 2014).

Chapter 2

[3] Courtney Subramian, "Google Study Gets Employees to Stop Eating So Many M&Ms," TIME.com, September 3, 2013, https://newsfeed.time.com/2013/09/03/google-study-gets-employees-to-stop-eating-so-many-mms/, last accessed November 30, 2022.

[4] Michalowicz, *Profit First*

Chapter 5

[5] Michalowicz, *Profit First*

Chapter 9

[6] Ramsey Solutions editors, "The National Study of Millionaires," RamseySolutions.com, https://www.ramseysolutions.com/retirement/the-national-study-of-millionaires-research, last accessed November 30, 2022.

Chapter 11

[7] Kasey Compton, *Fix This Next for Healthcare Providers* (Somerset, KY: Kasey R Compton and Associates, 2021).

Chapter 12

[8] Department of the Treasury, Internal Revenue Service, "Publication 970, Tax Benefits for Education," February 15, 2022, https://www.irs.gov/pub/irs-pdf/p970.pdf, last accessed November 30, 2022.

Chapter 13

[9] Alexander Huls, "The Key to Managing Profit and Cash Flow for Your Small Business and Knowing the Difference Between the Two," Small Biz Ahead at TheHartford.com, published August 10, 2016, updated August 22, 2022, https://sba.thehartford.com/finance/managing-profit-cash-flow/, last accessed November 30, 2022.

[10] Dan Sullivan and Dr. Benjamin Hardy, *Who Not How: The Formula to Achieve Bigger Goals Through Accelerating Teamwork* (Carlsbad, CA: Hay House Business, 2020).

ACKNOWLEDGMENTS

WRITING *PROFIT FIRST FOR THERAPISTS* was a labor of love. I knew that writing a book would be challenging, but nothing could have prepared me for just how hard it was. I have so many people to thank for making it possible.

To my husband, Mick Herres: This book would still be a dream if it weren't for you. You are so much better a spouse than I ever wished for, and we truly bring out the best in each other. You paved the way as the first entrepreneur in our duo, and you have been patient and supportive as I make my own way as a small business owner. It's not always easy being married to an entrepreneur, but you have figured out when I need advice and when I need you to "just listen." Our roles have changed many times over the last fifteen years, and I couldn't be more grateful for your love and support.

To our beautiful children, Paul, Rebecca, and Jackson: You are the light of my life. Thank you for believing in me and for your encouragement through the ups and downs of writing. You can achieve anything in life if you just keep going.

To my ride or die, my sister and best friend, Stephanie Chenevert: I started this project at such a difficult time in our lives, and I will forever cherish the time we got to spend together. Your unwavering support helped me through in ways you'll never know.

To my mom, Danielle Vallee. Much of this book was written while caring for my mother during her brave fight with ALS. I wish she had seen my book come to life because I know how happy it would make her. I am forever grateful for the years we had together and the love (and fear) of entrepreneurship she instilled in me.

To my dad and stepmom, Bernard and Claudette Chenevert: Thank you for being the steady presence I have always needed. There is no doubt that my love of personal finance and saving comes from you.

To AJ Harper and Laura Stone: The way you lead your Top Three Workshop students through the writing process is pure magic. I can't imagine trying to do this without your support, encouragement, and kindness.

To Mike Michalowicz and the Profit First Professionals Team: Profit First changed my business and gave me the courage to be a small business owner when my internal narrative made me doubt I could. Profit First has forever changed my family tree. I am honored to customize this amazing system for the mental health industry and further the Profit First Professionals' mission to eradicate entrepreneurial poverty.

To Abby Henning, my book launch manager and constant cheerleader: You have kept me on track and on task and have gracefully orchestrated all the logistics for this book to make it into the world. You never doubted my ability to get this book completed, and I greatly appreciate all the gentle "nudging" you had to do during this process.

Finally, to my entire team at GreenOak Accounting: I owe a tremendous debt of gratitude to you. You gave me the space and time to write this book by managing the day-to-day operations of the firm and taking great care of our clients each day. A special thank you to my leadership team (in alphabetical order): Kelly Andrewlevich, Carolyn Chrestman, Emily Grauerholz, Kelly Jewell, Jacquie Kiefer, and Heidi Stepzinski, I could not have done this without you. Thank you.

ABOUT THE AUTHOR

JULIE HERRES IS THE FOUNDER and CEO of GreenOak Accounting, a firm that exclusively serves therapists, psychologists, and counselors in private practice across the United States. Over the years, Julie and her team have worked with hundreds of private practice owners and developed serious knowledge about what makes a practice financially successful. GreenOak's goal is to help practice owners feel comfortable with the financial side of their businesses and have profitable practices. Some of the firm's biggest success stories were achieved through implementing Profit First.

Julie is an accountant and an enrolled agent (EA)*. She is also a speaker and the host of the *Therapy for Your Money* podcast.

FIND JULIE ONLINE

@julie.herres
www.julieherres.com
www.therapyforyourmoney.com
www.greenoakaccounting.com
www.profitfirstfortherapists.com

*While EAs are not as well-known as CPAs, this robust, tax-specific license allows accountants all the privileges afforded to CPAs, like representing clients before the IRS, filing tax returns, and much more. Both licenses denote knowledgeable, experienced professionals who are required to maintain high ethical standards. The primary difference between an EA and a CPA is that EAs specialize in taxation, while CPAs can specialize in taxation or other accounting areas such as financial audits, assurance, or corporate finance.